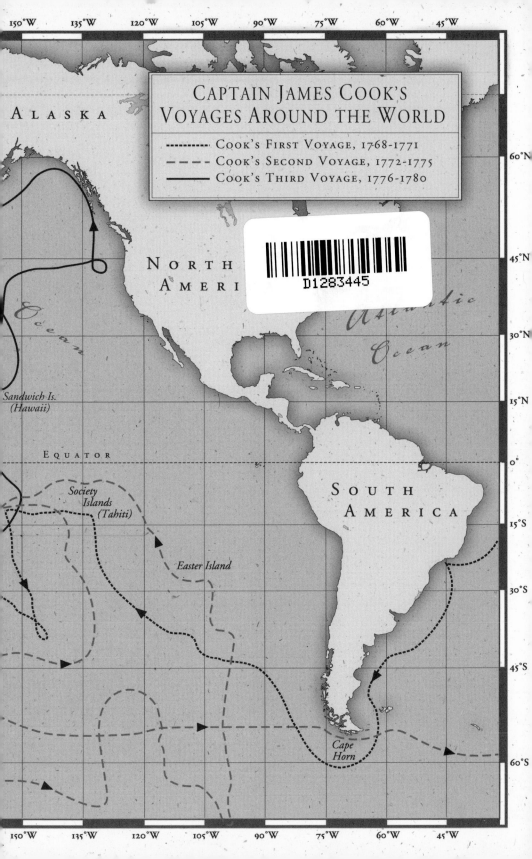

CAPTAIN JAMES COOK'S
VOYAGES AROUND THE WORLD

---------- COOK'S FIRST VOYAGE, 1768-1771
- - - - - COOK'S SECOND VOYAGE, 1772-1775
———— COOK'S THIRD VOYAGE, 1776-1780

ALASKA

NORTH AMERICA

Sandwich Is.
(Hawaii)

EQUATOR

Society
Islands
(Tahiti)

Easter Island

SOUTH AMERICA

Cape
Horn

Ocean

Atlantic Ocean

D1283445

Books of Merit

Scurvy

SCURVY

STEPHEN R. BOWN

HOW A SURGEON, A MARINER, AND A GENTLEMAN SOLVED THE GREATEST MEDICAL MYSTERY OF THE AGE OF SAIL

THOMAS ALLEN PUBLISHERS

TORONTO

National Library of Canada Cataloguing in Publication

Bown, Stephen R.
Scurvy : how a surgeon, a mariner, and a gentleman solved the
greatest medical mystery of the age of sail / Stephen R. Bown.

Includes index.

ISBN 0-88762-130-9

1. Scurvy—History.   I. Title.

RC627.S36B69 2003   616.3'94'009   C2003-901998-5

Jacket and text design: Gordon Robertson
Editor: Jim Gifford
Maps: John Lightfoot
Jacket images: (ship) "Nelson's HMS *Victory*," by Alfredo Carmelo,
courtesy the Carmelo estate; (lemon) www.fotosearch.com

Published by Thomas Allen Publishers,
a division of Thomas Allen & Son Limited,
145 Front Street East, Suite 209,
Toronto, Ontario M5A 1E3 Canada

www.thomas-allen.com

Canada Council
for the Arts

ONTARIO ARTS COUNCIL
CONSEIL DES ARTS DE L'ONTARIO

The publisher gratefully acknowledges the support of
the Ontario Arts Council for its publishing program.

We acknowledge the support of the Canada Council for the Arts, which
last year invested $20.3 million in writing and publishing throughout Canada.

We acknowledge the Government of Ontario through the
Ontario Media Development Corporation's Ontario Book Initiative.

07 06 05 04 03   1 2 3 4 5

Printed and bound in Canada

Contents

Scurvy

PROLOGUE:
A MEDICAL MYSTERY

---

scur·vy *['skurvi] n., adj. (-vi·er, -vi·est).*
-n. Pathology.
a disease caused by lack of vitamin C, characterized by
swollen and bleeding gums, livid spots on the skin, and
prostration. Scurvy used to be common among sailors
when they had little to eat except bread and salt meat.
-adj.
low; mean; contemptible: a scurvy fellow, a scurvy trick.
scur·vi·ly, *adv.,* **scur·vi·ness,** *n.*

ARTHUR JAMES WAS TOO WEAK to scamper up the masts and rigging, useless even for hauling on a rope or mending a damaged sail. Reluctantly ordered below deck, he crawled into the bowels of the ship, where the men's hammocks were strung up, and joined the others who had succumbed to the insidious illness. The worst of them were hideously drawn, feverish, dreamy, and insensible; their skin was like paper covered in blotches of ink as they lay shrunken and gap-toothed in their hammocks, swaying with the motion of the ship. They were listless and morose in their misery and despair, moaning under the dim light from a few oil lamps, patiently awaiting death from this most feared of all maritime diseases. Some cried because they were cold, others because they were hungry and thirsty. They could not eat because their mouths were in ruins—swollen gums, brown and spongy, grown over their wobbly teeth. Their breath rattled in their chests and their eyes were dull and unfocused.

Soon James's shipmates began to die, in such numbers that there were scarcely any strong enough to sew them into their hammocks and give them a proper farewell before pitching them overboard. Corpses lay in the fetid compartments belowdecks, stiff, blue, and shrunken, gnawed on by rats and abandoned by their comrades. Others sprawled about the deck until someone pushed them overboard. The ship left a trail of bobbing corpses in its wake as it limped into a safe port on Juan Fernandez Island, off the coast of Chile, where the crew desperately hoped to find fresh fruit and vegetables.

Arthur James was one of the hundreds of men who wasted away and died of the dreaded scurvy while Commodore George Anson's flagship, *Centurion*, rounded Cape Horn in 1741 on a mission to harass Spanish shipping in the Pacific Ocean. Of the nearly two thousand men who set off from Portsmouth the previous year in five warships and a sloop, only about two hundred ever saw home again, the vast bulk of them perishing horribly from scurvy. What happened on Anson's voyage is considered one of the worst seaborne medical disasters of all time. It sickened and appalled the English public and aroused the consternation of naval authorities concerned with the loss of the astronomically expensive warships. It sparked a golden age of scurvy research in England that would see the distemper practically cured, if not fully understood, before the century was out.

Scurvy was responsible for more deaths at sea than storms, ship-wreck, combat, and all other diseases combined. Historians have conservatively estimated that more than two million sailors perished from scurvy during the Age of Sail—a time period that began with Columbus's voyages across the Atlantic and ended with the development of steam power and its adaptation for engines on ships in the mid-nineteenth century. Like a constant but irritating and occasionally violent companion, it had sailed with virtually every major voyage of discovery, from Jacques Cartier to Vasco da Gama to Francis Drake. Explorers feared it, the merchants of the Dutch and English East India companies feared it, and by the eighteenth century Europe's national navies feared it. It was not uncommon for a proud and lumbering warship to slide to sea from Portsmouth or sally forth from Brest with more than seven hundred mariners and return months later with only three hundred sickly wretches—the unlucky others perishing horribly from the "grey killer" during the months at sea, the life slowly sucked from them on a diet of salt pork, biscuit, and grog.

Scurvy is a hideous and frightful affliction by which the body's connective tissue degenerates, resulting in bleeding gums, wobbly teeth, rot-reeking breath, anemic lethargy, physical weakness, the opening of old wounds, and the separating of once healed broken bones. Untreated, it leads to a slow, agonizing, and inevitable death. Although it is associated with the sea and sailors, scurvy appeared regularly in northern countries during winter months, during sieges, in prisons, or when harvests failed—anytime and anywhere people have subsisted on foods insufficient in ascorbic acid, vitamin C. But on long sea voyages it became virtually an occupational disease for sailors, because they had no means to carry fresh foods rich in the vital vitamin. Although the bulk of scurvy-ridden sailors usually recovered and returned to active duty, they would often succumb to the disease many times during the course of their naval lives, at great expense in medical treatment and with disastrous implications when ships sailed short-handed.

Scurvy had puzzled physicians and philosophers since the time of the ancient Greeks. The Hippocratic theoretical foundation that all illness stemmed from an imbalance in the four bodily humours—the black bile, the yellow bile, the blood, and the phlegm—resulted in medical reasoning and treatments that today seem disconnected from reality. The greatest medical minds of the era put forth new theories and proposals. Dozens of tracts were written on scurvy, claiming such varied causes for the distemper as foul vapours, dampness and cold, an excess of black bile, laziness, copper poisoning, the Dutch method of refining salt, inherited predisposition, blocked perspiration, and divine disfavour.

Common folk cures were as varied, bizarre, and optimistic as the motivations for the multitudes of voyages. Typical cures included purging with salt water, bleeding, eating sulphuric acid or vinegar, smearing mercury paste onto the open sores, or increasing sailors' workload in the belief that the disease was caused by indolence and sloth. Not surprisingly, the cure often proved as deadly as the disease. What was surprising, however, were the truly effective suggestions that cropped up now and then, such as James Lancaster's sixteenth-century recommendation to scorbutic sailors to eat lemons, a fruit modern researchers have shown to be high in vitamin C. Somehow these practical and useful propositions were overshadowed by other, less effective ideas, or were dismissed because of impracticality or cost. Scurvy could not be cured because it could not be understood.

Because of the difficulties and limitations of food preservation, scurvy reached epidemic proportions during the Age of Sail. It was a primarily European problem that cropped up when ships had grown large enough to ply the world's oceans on voyages lasting months or years, often with infrequent landings because of an inability to accurately navigate or a fear of hostile peoples. When crews did land, they had no knowledge to determine which local plants were poisonous and which were edible. Britain, France, Spain, and the Netherlands were the nations with the ships and knowledge to undertake lengthy deep-sea voyages or to mount naval blockades of enemy ports, and hence the nations that suffered the most from scurvy.

Millions of men perished horribly during these centuries of early seafaring, destroyed directly by scurvy or indirectly when the weakened state of crews meant ships were swamped in monstrous storms or ran aground on jagged reefs or were unable to defend themselves from pirates or enemy ships. Despite scurvy's horrendous impact on maritime exploration and global trade, it never achieved the death toll of other dreaded diseases, such as the bubonic plague, smallpox, or malaria. For most of its history, scurvy merely lurked in the background like a shadow, influencing events in a subtle and unpredictable manner, culling sailors and stunting maritime enterprise. But during one brief period of time in the late eighteenth century, the hinges of history turned on the discovery of a cure for scurvy—and the timely discovery of that cure changed the course of world events. At that time, a convergence of naval technology, greater geographical knowledge of the world, and intense international conflict conspired to elevate the cure from the solution to a deadly yet predictable irritant to a vital factor determining the destiny of nations.

Throughout most of the eighteenth century, England and France, with a series of shifting alliances, were grappling for pre-eminence in Europe. Apart from several brief intervals of official peace, the era was dominated by war: the War of the Spanish Succession, the War of Jenkins's Ear and the Austrian Succession, the Seven Years' War, the War of American Independence, the French Revolution, and the

Napoleonic Wars. Control of the seas would prove to be crucial in determining the outcome of these conflicts. After centuries of half-hearted questing for a solution to the greatest disease of the Age of Sail, the terrible danger and cost of not finding a cure was becoming all too apparent—to ignore scurvy any longer was to make a wild gamble with national security. The time and effort required to put into port and transport scorbutic sailors to and from hospitals were a significant liability in times of war, when men and ships were direly important and in short supply. The plague of the sea sapped a navy's strength, both financially and in terms of manpower, and had a direct impact on a nation's ability to defend itself. Moreover, who-ever defeated scurvy, the Achilles heel of all the European navies, would acquire a significant strategic advantage—the ability to remain at sea for longer periods of time.

It was a trio of individuals in Britain who converged to lift the veil of obscurity from scurvy—a bookish surgeon named James Lind, the famed mariner and sea captain James Cook, and an influ-ential physician and gentleman named Sir Gilbert Blane. It was a long road to a simple solution, but in the eighteenth century, that solution was far from obvious. At that time, despite several centuries of suffering, scurvy was still the greatest medical mystery of the age, a puzzle that continued to baffle mariners and medical theorists. From the bewildering fog of conflicting ideas, Lind, Cook, and Blane, working independently over several decades, overcame not only the sheer magnitude of the problem but the preposterous theoretical foundations of medicine, a confusing array of other ail-ments with similar symptoms, bureaucratic intransigence, and the unknown and fickle properties of one of the most promising cures. They proved that scurvy was a disease of chemistry and food—not vapours and viruses. Although seemingly obvious from a modern perspective, scurvy's cure remained elusive for so long with good reason—its seeds were in the very nature of our biology, and the germination of those seeds was in the nature of early maritime enterprise and life at sea. Scurvy lurked on ships long before they ever left port, waiting to appear under the right set of conditions—conditions that a sea life hastened.

The defeat of scurvy was one of the great medical and socio-military advances of the era, a discovery on par with the accurate calculation of longitude at sea, the creation of the smallpox vaccination, or the development of steam power. The convoluted and bizarre story of the quest for scurvy's cure turns around an unusual quirk of human biology, the confusion of early medical theory, international politics, the yawning gulf between individuals caused by European class structure, and finally military necessity. How the cure for scurvy was found and lost and finally found again at an important juncture in the history of the world is one of the great mysteries of the age.

I

THE
EIGHTEENTH-CENTURY
SEAFARING WORLD:
THE AGE OF SCURVY

AN ENGLISH SAILOR RELAXED in an alehouse with companions after a long voyage from the West Indies. After over a year away, he wanted to celebrate his safe return. The merchant ship had returned to Portsmouth with a load of spices and exotic wood. It had been a good run; the winds and weather had been fair and the incidence of disease low. Still, he was lucky to have survived, and several of his fellow mariners had not. He had been ashore for several days, paid out by his captain, and he was enjoying his liberty, spending his hard-earned coin. Downing the last of many mugs of ale, he was surprised to find a shilling at the bottom. Something did not seem right, but he had had much to drink this night. Blessing his good fortune, he pocketed the coin, bade farewell to his drinking companions, and staggered from the crowded interior out onto the dark street, heading for a flophouse. He was followed from the alehouse. Three more men waited for him in the shadows. Armed with clubs and with stern expressions on their faces, they surrounded him, leaving no room for escape. With dawning horror, the sailor realized his predicament. He felt the coin in his pocket, the King's Shilling, and belatedly knew that it had been placed in his drink, and that the men of the press gang would swear he had gladly taken it and agreed to join a ship's company. The men grabbed him and dragged him, protesting and struggling until a thump on his head silenced him, towards the harbour. A man-of-war had sailed into port and was looking for recruits.

The sailor, like countless others, had now joined the Royal Navy. Life was so hard in the navy, the chance of death so high, and the demand for human fuel so insatiable during times of war that sailors in sufficient quantities to navigate the lumbering warships would rarely sign on voluntarily. It was far safer and more rewarding to sail on merchant ships. The navy's need for men was at least double, perhaps triple, the number of able-bodied seamen who willingly served. Ships were chronically short-handed. Offering a bonus to new recruits failed to provide the needed seamen. A quota system, whereby each county was responsible for furnishing to the navy a specified number of sailors, failed. Beseeching men to do their duty for their country also failed. Short of raising wages and improving conditions, the navy could guarantee a ready supply of sailors only by taking them by force.

Famous fighting captains who were believed to have good luck, and who could boast of a good chance of prize money from capturing enemy ships, could announce their need for sailors on posters about town and receive a stream of able seamen eager to join the ship's company. But most captains had to resort to the notorious Impress Service. As a consequence, in eighteenth-century Britain men frequently disappeared from seaport towns and villages. Wandering alone one evening, they would be clubbed, dragged aboard a ship in port, and "recruited" into the navy. Wives were often left wondering what had become of their husbands, and children of their fathers. Many were never seen by their families again. Press gangs patrolled the narrow warrens and alleys of the poor dockside quarters, searching for anyone alone or too drunk to flee, sailors preferably, but during wartime any reasonably able-bodied men would do. Sometimes the new recruits were rounded up by land-based agents of the Impress Service, who were paid a commission to deliver men to whichever ship lay in port. On other occasions, captains were empowered to search for men themselves, employing gangs usually consisting of four stout seamen armed with clubs and—officially, at least—one lieutenant armed with a cutlass, ostensibly used to impress bystanders with his martial appearance and social respectability. They would sally forth from the ship after darkness in pursuit of their quarry.

Many of the "recruits" brought in by the press gangs had little or no experience at sea. Although officially the Impress Service had the legal right to deliver only "seamen, seafaring men and persons whose occupations or callings are to work in vessels and boats upon rivers," on short notice nearly anyone would do (providing they weren't influential or wealthy). Once shipboard, the men were subject to the law of the sea, and to leave was desertion. Desertion was punishable by death. The impressed sailor, if he was lucky, could look forward to years of harsh, brutal service at sea. If he was unlucky, he would die without ever setting foot on his native soil again. The naval historian Sir Harold Scott wryly observed that "it was a curious anomaly: the security of citizens depended on the Fleet. The manning of the Fleet was, therefore, a prime necessity, and the citizens—the pressed men among them, at least—were 'made slaves' in order to keep them free." Up to a third of a ship's company could be made up of men pressed from land or taken from incoming merchant ships.

The majority of the men newly rounded up by the Impress Service, as might be supposed, were not the pick of the country; they were primarily spindle-legged landlubbers, vagrants, or tramps in the

The Royal Navy needed at least double the number of able-bodied seamen who would willingly serve. In eighteenth-century Britain men frequently disappeared from seaport towns and villages. Wandering alone they were clubbed, dragged aboard ships in port, and "recruited" into the navy. Many were never seen by their families again.

poorest of physical health. The press gang might also roust out the sick, malnourished, or elderly, or receive from local magistrates convicts who were given a choice between severe punishment or the king's service. Seamen aboard incoming merchant ships were also at risk of impressment. The Royal Navy stopped these ships and claimed any men on board, preferably those who had already served in the navy, beyond the absolute minimum needed to sail the vessel. But not all men in the navy were pressed or convicts. Many joined willingly: for a chance to see the world or out of patriotic duty. But some of those inclined to volunteer would do so only at the end of a particularly harsh winter, when a secure place to sleep, regular, if paltry, pay, and the promise of a daily meal overcame their fear of possible death and the inevitable loss of freedom.

Once shipboard, duty was paramount. Discipline was strict, authoritarian, and often violent. There was a great social gulf between the commissioned officers and the common crew, and the captain was a virtual dictator while at sea. It was an age of severe punishments; life was cheap, and the concept of workers' rights lay in the distant future. Even minor crimes such as theft would be dealt with harshly, usually by flogging with the dreaded cat-o'-nine-tails. Crimes that seem relatively innocuous, such as disrespect for a superior officer or inattention to duty, were very serious shipboard, where the lives of all depended on each other; these could be punished with a dozen or even a hundred or more lashes—sometimes enough to kill a man. Because there were no standards for punishment, individual captains wielded great power over their crews. Some were known for being brutal martinets, lashing and beating sailors far in excess of their crimes, while others rarely resorted to the lash. Another common but lesser punishment was known as starting; an officer would whack a sailor with his cane if he thought he was moving too slowly or was showing belligerence to authority. Lashing and starting were most prevalent on ships with great numbers of convicts and pressed men, and they created a tense and gloomy atmosphere that was poor for morale and health. The threat of corporal punishment hung over every man's head.

Most of the newly pressed recruits in the navy were not mariners and had never been to sea before. Although they all lived and slept together and ate the same food, there was a hierarchy even amongst the common sailors. While a contingent of skilled able seamen performed all the difficult tasks, such as climbing the rigging and setting the sails, the unskilled men, sickly or weak, were good only for hauling on a rope or swabbing the decks. Not only did they have no nautical skill or inclination, but many of the new recruits, and especially those who had recently come from prison, were already afflicted with one of the many illnesses common in the Age of Sail. Even the able seamen on the majority of ships were barely fit for the harsh realities of life at sea, and conditions became worse when the pressed sailors (morose and melancholy at their dreadful fate) and the convicts (delirious from typhus or dysentery) were taken on board and housed with the rest of the crew, thereby spreading discontent and disease throughout the ship's company.

Mariners in the eighteenth century suffered from a bewildering array of ailments, diseases, and dietary deficiencies, such that it was next to impossible for surgeons or physicians to accurately separate the symptoms of one from those of another. Niacin deficiency caused lunacy and convulsions, thiamin deficiency caused beriberi, and vitamin-A deficiency caused night blindness. Syphilis, malaria, rickets, smallpox, tuberculosis, yellow fever, venereal diseases, dysentery, and food poisoning were constant companions. Typhus, or typhoid fever, was common on every ship. Spread by infected lice in the frequently shared and rarely cleaned bedding, typhus was so prevalent in the navy that it was known as "ship's fever" or "gaol fever." Man-of-war and merchantman, both were a cozy den for disease.

Life shipboard was not conducive to curing or avoiding any of these varied ailments, and indeed was an ideal environment for spreading them. The sailor's wooden world was infested with refuse, trash, rotting flesh, urine, and vomit. The mariners were either crammed into their quarters like sardines in a box or slept, occasionally in good weather, sprawled like hounds on the deck. The holds were crammed with vermin, festering and spoiled provisions, and in some cases rotting corpses. On English and Dutch ships, the primarily Protestant dead sailors were wrapped in their hammocks and pitched overboard—with proper ceremony, naturally. But on the ships from Catholic countries such as France and Spain, the decaying bodies were stowed in the gravel of the hold, mouldering for perhaps months until the ships returned to home port and the dead could be buried in their native soil. The ships always leaked, and pumps could never keep the water out entirely, so the ballast of gravel or sand became incredibly putrid. Ventilation was poor and the bilge gases so noxious that it was extremely hazardous for carpenters to go below to work in the hold. The stench was unbearable, and occasionally men suffocated from inhaling the fumes.

Sanitary conditions aboard ships, and particularly the warships of national navies, were as bad as or worse than the filthiest slums then in London, Amsterdam, Paris, or Seville. The cramped, stifling, congested forecastle, where the crew slept, was dark and dingy. The air was clouded with noxious bilge gasses and congested with the sweet, cloying reek of rot and sweat. Sailors slept in dirty bedding and wore the same vermin-infested rags for months on end. The British naval commander Frederick Chamier wrote in *The Life of a Sailor* of his first days on a ship in port as a young midshipman during the Napoleonic Wars. "Dirty women," he wrote, "the objects of sailors' affections, with beer cans in hand, were everywhere conspicuous: the shrill whistle squeaked, and the noise of the boatswain and his mate rattled like thunder in my ears; the deck was dirty, slippery and wet; the smells abominable; the whole sight disgusting."

Overcrowding contributed to the unsanitary conditions and the spread of disease. The largest battleships, weighing approximately 2,500 tons and boasting 120 great guns, yet only several hundred feet long, could house more than a thousand men. Large crews were needed because, in addition to manning the sails, eight to twelve men were required to operate each gun. Because of the high mortality rates, navy ships were oversupplied with men. The ships themselves were extremely valuable; they took years to build and required two thousand to three thousand mature oak trees each. It was unthinkable to lose a ship of the line because of a lack of manpower to sail it properly. Consequently, a warship requiring a normal complement of a thousand sailors would weigh anchor and depart for sea with many hundreds more crammed aboard. Perhaps five hundred men at any given time slung their hammocks between the great guns, in a compartment no more than 50 feet wide and 150 feet long. Sleeping, coughing, and sneezing with as little as fourteen inches between men encouraged the spread of infectious and contagious diseases. The overcrowding itself was as great a cause of disease as the unsanitary conditions. One of the great and sad ironies of the age was that naval authorities increased the number of men on ships in anticipation of replacing those who died. The overcrowding increased the deaths, however, leading naval authorities to strive for even greater numbers at the start of every voyage. It was a vicious circle that in the 1700s took a terrible toll of human life from all the major seafaring nations, leaving ships dangerously undermanned at sea and occasionally crippling entire fleets.

A warship preparing for sea was a hive of chaotic activity. All hands scuttled about the dock and deck, hauling on rough hemp ropes and hoisting provisions and stores across the crack of water that separated the ship from the provisioning barge. They swabbed the upper deck, scrubbed the gun decks with vinegar, and fumigated the lower compartments with smoking brimstone to cleanse the malignant airs that were believed to be the cause of most ailments.

They lowered the wrapped bundles and barrels into the gaping maw of the hatch, stowing everything in the dank bowels of the ship, including carpenters' tools, cutlasses and other weapons for close combat, kegs of gunpowder, mounds of cannonballs, spare spars, dozens of sails, vast coils of rope, tubs of tar, casks of grease, canisters of paint, cords of wood, and buckets of coal.

But perhaps most impressive were the mountains of food needed to feed hundreds of mariners for months or years without replenishing. Although ships frequently purchased supplies from local ports, these could not be counted on for price or availability, and particularly in the navy, ships had to be prepared to carry out orders at a moment's notice. Once the provisions had been lowered onto the deck, the barefoot, pigtailed foremast jacks leapt to roll to the central hatch great oak barrels of salted beef, pork, and fish; kegs of English beer and West Indian rum; back-breaking burlap sacks of flour, dried peas, and oats; monstrous wheels of cheese; great blocks of butter; casks of molasses; and a huge quantity of hardtack cakes. The victualling yards of the major European ports were all well supplied to support departing ships on short notice.

The standard naval diet varied only slightly over the centuries and only slightly between the various European nations. Ships' provisions were limited by what could be preserved or stored for months at a time without going bad. Salt beef or pork, dried peas or grains, or ship's biscuit were standard fare from the time of the Spanish Armada in the sixteenth century through the period when Dutch merchants piloted their way to Indonesia (the Dutch East Indies) to the era of the great naval battles between France and England in the eighteenth century. The Spanish fed on more oil and pickled vegetables, the Dutch on more sauerkraut and dunderfunk (fried biscuit with lard and molasses), but on the whole the sailors' diet was remarkably constant between nations—it simply reflected the only items that could survive for any length of time. On foreign shores, items such as rice were substituted for flour, wine for beer, and other hard liquors for rum. From 1757 on, the British navy issued a vital and innovative substance known as portable soup. Essentially it was a dried soup made from "all the offals of oxen killed in London for the use of the navy," mixed with salt and a few vegetables. It resembled large slabs of glue and could be stored for years.

A typical weekly menu for the average sailor was as follows:

Biscuit	1 lb. daily
Salt beef	2 lb. twice weekly
Salt pork	1 lb. twice weekly
Dried fish	2 oz. thrice weekly
Butter	2 oz. thrice weekly
Cheese	4 oz. thrice weekly
Peas	8 oz. four days per week
Beer	1 gal. daily

To this weekly menu were often added raisins, barley meal, sugar, and perhaps dried apples or pears. More expensive provisions were allocated to the ship's company and were to be administered to the sick under the watchful eye of the surgeon. These could include currants, tamarinds, sago, almonds, garlic, mace, and nutmeg. The men were divided into messes of six to eight companions, and they ate between the great guns at tables suspended from above deck with rope. Breakfast, dinner, and supper were all similar, with the beer, grog, or wine served up just after the men had eaten. The monotonous, crude, and nearly unpalatable food was served in great quantity, though, and would have amounted to nearly four thousand calories per day—more than adequate for the hard labour of the men—if not for the fact that it was sorely deficient in certain key vitamins. But the problem with the naval diet went far beyond its vitamin deficiencies. After prolonged time at sea, the provisions began to rot.

Ships were built almost exclusively from wood. While this had advantages, such as increased buoyancy, the wood quickly became waterlogged, creating a permanently damp and cold environment. Men lived in the damp, worked belowdecks in the damp, slept in the damp, and ate food that was continuously stored in the damp. When it rained and during rough seas, they had no means of drying themselves after their watch. Although the ship's biscuit room was sometimes specially lined with tin and caulked to keep it as dry as possible, biscuit being a staple of the sea diet and particularly susceptible to mould, it too eventually became waterlogged, so that the hardtack grew heavy and green about the edges on prolonged voyages. The peas, oats, and flour likewise began to moulder.

The Scottish naval surgeon and physician James Lind wrote that the naval food in his experience consisted of "putrid beef, rancid pork, mouldy biscuits and flour." The naval captain and later first Lord of the Admiralty Sir George Anson complained that some of the "fresh" beef he acquired in Brazil on his famous voyage in 1741 was "bruized and stinking," and he threw it overboard. Later in the voyage, his surgeon, Pascoe Thomas, described the sea rations as almost inedible: the biscuit was "so much worm-eaten, it was scarce anything but Dust," while the salt pork "was likewise very rusty and rotten." James Patten, a surgeon aboard Cook's second voyage, remarked that "our bread was . . . both musty and mouldy, and at the same time swarming with two different sorts of little brown grubs, the *circulio granorius* (or weevil) and the *dermestes paniceus. . . .* Their larvas, or maggots, were found in such quantities in the pease-soup, as if they had been strewed over our plates on purpose, so that we could not avoid swallowing some of them in every spoonful we took."

The damp, dark, and unventilated environment was ideal for vermin, which infested nearly all the food eaten shipboard. Admiral Raigersfield wrote in the late 1700s that "the biscuit that was served to the ship's company was so light, that when you tipped it on the table, it almost fell into dust, and thereout numerous insects, called weevils, crawled; they were bitter to the taste, and a sure indication that the biscuit had lost its nutritious particles; if instead of these weevils, large white maggots with black heads made their appearance (these were called bargemen in the Navy), then the biscuit was considered to be only in its first state of decay; these maggots were fat and cold to the taste, but not bitter." Sailors were known to be particularly suspicious of hardtack that contained no weevils or maggots, believing it to be too bad even for these ever-prevalent pests. One of the most nutritious foods found shipboard, a food that was at least marginally less revolting than the weevils and bargemen, were the rats. With a secure food supply, the rats grew plump over time and were reputedly "full as good as rabbits, although not so large." They were known as millers, because they were white with flour dust. After months of living on sea rations, for many sailors rats were the only source of fresh meat.

Salt beef or pork, the staple of a sea diet, was known as sea junk or sea horse (and periodically the indistinguishable tough grey meat was indeed horse). After several months at sea, it stank horribly when taken from the brine, was riddled with maggots, or had dried and hardened beyond the ability of the saltwater soaking to reconstitute it. The method of preparing meals also added woe to a sailor's life. A day in advance of each mealtime, the cook removed the meat from the brine in the barrel and slung it into several large nets attached to a rope. These he brought to the stern of the ship and, after tying the rope to a cleat, flung overboard. The meat would then "wash" in the sea as it was dragged behind the ship, cleansing it of excess salt for up to half a day. Fresh water was too valuable and scarce, particularly after months at sea when supplies were dwindling, for soaking meat. The meat was then boiled in a great copper vat of sea water, fresh water again being too scarce even for cooking. The salt was so strong and concentrated on the cooked meat that if it was not eaten quickly, white crystals would form on the surface. It burned the sailors' mouths as they ate, increasing their thirst for the carefully rationed supply of water. Instead of water to quench their thirst, they drank beer or grog or wine, and as a blessed respite by the late eighteenth century, tea or cocoa.

One of the few special treats available to the crew were the fatty dregs of the boiled salt meat, called slush. Because it was usually in great demand, it was the cook's special privilege to claim the slush and sell it to augment his wages. Sailors would smear it on hardtack or mix it with their oatmeal or work it into their clothes to water-proof them. Occasionally the cook would ration it to the ship to grease the ropes or canvas. But usually it was purchased and eaten. Unfortunately the slush, although high in calories, contributed to malabsorption of the nutrients of other foods, because the copper acetate from the pots dissolved in the fat.

Ship's cheese quickly went rancid, cloaking the entire ship in a cloying cloud of noxious stench. If it didn't turn putrid, the cheese hardened like a rock, so sailors carved it with their knives into buttons for their clothing. Vast quantities of cheese were hove overboard, considered too foul even for seasoned sailors accustomed to corrupted sea horse. In general, more food was spoiled than was eaten, because there was no refrigeration and no other entirely effective means of preserving food beyond salting and drying. Even the fresh water became putrid or briny, so the standard drink on ships was alcohol—beer at the start of a voyage, before it spoiled, then wine mixed with water or diluted hard liquor. Alcoholism was rampant amongst the crew and the officers, and it was not uncommon for surgeons to be treating sailors who broke bones tumbling from the rigging while drunk.

Although Admiralty victualling authorities were supposed to oversee the quality and quantity of provisions, victuallers were known to provide shortened quantities of food, or to supply poor-quality meat from old or sick animals. Occasionally they didn't bother to rinse the meat after butchering, so that blood and other animal fluids leaked into the brine and spoiled it. It was not uncommon for provisions to be several years old before even being loaded onto a ship, and then months more passed before the casks were opened. Before a ship left port, much of its provisions were past their prime. On paper the food might have seemed nutritious, but with ships in port serving up sea rations to the men for months before sailing, even high-quality provisions deteriorated so as to be nearly unpalatable after a short time at sea. Furthermore, because of the great number of men packed onto warships in port, pursers were less inclined to purchase the more expensive and wholesome fresh foods. After subsisting for months on maggot-infested ship's biscuit made putrid by storage, briny, unwholesome water, mouldy cheese, roach-ridden porridge, and stale beer, the crews became weakened and succumbed to an array of illnesses. From a modern perspective, the substances ladled out to the sailors in the eighteenth century would hardly be considered food, although it was often better and of greater quantity than the food available to many of the poor on land.

When a ship weighed anchor and put to sea, the workload of the average sailor increased dramatically. Even with hundreds of extra hands crowded on board, there was an endless cycle of duties. A warship at sea had to be manned around the clock, in foul weather as well as fair. The ship didn't shut down for the night or tie up at a dock; it needed an equal number of men at all times, hour after hour, day after day, without a break. If a ship did need to get to port, because of disease, an ailing captain, or storm damage, it could take days, even weeks, with men constantly on duty. A day in the British navy was divided into seven watches—five of four hours in length and two shorter "dog watches" of two hours each. Other nations had a similar system for dividing the responsibilities aboard ship. The seven periods of duty in each twenty-four-hour day were divided between two shifts, the starboard watch and the larboard (port) watch. The alternating shifts meant that the men never slept for more than four hours at a time (in reality less, since socializing and eating were done during time off duty). This routine, however, applied only to periods of calm sailing. During storms, or while fleeing an enemy ship or preparing for combat, mariners laboured long hours in the cold and damp, sometimes for days without much sleep. Not to do so would have resulted in the foundering or loss of the ship and perhaps of their lives.

In addition to disease and corporal punishment, there were innumerable other ways for the average sailor to be maimed or killed during the Age of Sail, when the only thing powering the mighty ships was muscle and wind. He could slip and tumble from the rigging onto the deck and his bones crushed. He could be swept overboard in a storm and drown. The skin could be flayed off his hands from rope burn. During battle, he could be shot with guns, have his feet or a leg pulverized by the kickback of his own great cannon (which lobbed twenty-four- or thirty-two-pound balls of iron), or be mangled by flying cannonballs from an enemy ship. Shrapnel caused gaping splinter wounds, while exploding black powder would severely burn him. It would have been a rare sailor who didn't show the scars and wounds of his profession. "In consequence of what they [seamen] undergo," wrote the Scottish physician Sir Gilbert Blane in the 1790s, "they are in general short lived, and have their constitutions worn out ten years before the rest of the laborious part of mankind. A seaman, at the age of forty-five, if shown to a person not accustomed to be among them, would be taken by his looks to be fifty-five, or even on the borders of sixty."

While the average sailor was in poor health and suffering from malnutrition and a varying array of illnesses, and the sea life was harsh and physically and psychologically demanding, the cruellest fate of all was that each and every aspect of a sailor's working and living conditions conspired to bring on the greatest maritime disease of all, the dreaded scurvy.

Although after months at sea the entire ship's company would eventually be afflicted with scurvy, it was the common sailors who showed the earliest and most severe symptoms. Even after prolonged time at sea, the officers seldom fell prey to scurvy to the same extent as the crew, and the disease was often thought of as an illness particularly of the lower classes (reflected in such slang as "lazy skivvies" or "scurvy dogs"). The captain and ship's officers lived under more sanitary and less crowded conditions. They wore drier, cleaner clothes, ate better food, and slept more regularly. Although the navy officially supplied the captain and officers with the same sea rations as the crew, the officers always brought their own private preserves on board. These usually included fresh, dried, and pickled fruits and vegetables. They also kept live animals, which were slaughtered at sea for fresh meat. The decks of ships often had dozens of chickens, sheep, or pigs living in pens. On Cook's ship, the *Endeavour*, the same goat that had sailed on a previous Pacific voyage was "transferred to Cook so that South Sea coffee should still have its milk." Technically, the crew also were permitted to bring a store of personal supplies, but they rarely did so because the expense was beyond their meagre means and their pay was kept up to six months in arrears to prevent them from deserting.

The quest for a viable, portable, affordable alternative to a good diet and working conditions—something that would enable maritime expansion to continue without the horrendous losses—spanned centuries. In the 1590s Sir Richard Hawkins, who claimed to have personally witnessed more than ten thousand cases of scurvy during his life at sea, "wished some learned man would write of it, for it is the plague of the sea and Spoyle of Mariners." The renowned eighteenth-century essayist and critic Dr. Samuel Johnson waggishly

WAR SHIPS 18TH CENTURY

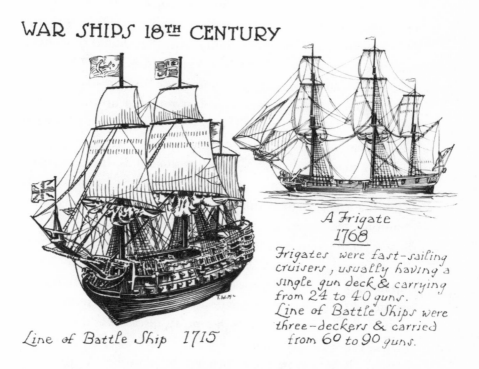

Line of Battle Ship   1715

A Frigate
1768

Frigates were fast-sailing cruisers, usually having a single gun deck & carrying from 24 to 40 guns.
Line of Battle Ships were three-deckers & carried from 60 to 90 guns.

Scurvy killed more sailors than storms, shipwrecks, and combat combined during the 18th century when only wind and muscle powered these majestic oaken hulks.

remarked, "Why, Sir, no man will be a sailor who has contrivance to get himself into a jail, for being in a ship is being in a jail with the chance of being drowned." Although Johnson was no doubt exaggerating to make a point, and life on land was also comparatively harsh, the record shows that he was not entirely off base. The sea life for European navy crew members was brutal. Drowning was of course an ever-present possibility, but what should really have concerned Johnson was scurvy. The Annual Register for 1763 tabulated the casualty list for British sailors in the Seven Years' War with France. Out of 184,899 men raised or rounded up for the war, 133,708 died from disease, primarily scurvy, while only 1,512 were killed in action.

While mariners died by the tens of thousands, the cocktail of other diseases and dietary deficiencies that afflicted the common sailors made it extremely difficult for medical men to isolate the symptoms and causes of, and therefore the cure for, the plague of the sea. People from around the world have a remarkable ability to survive in even the harshest environments. But a perpetually damp ship floating far from land for months at a time without fresh food was one of the most extreme environments possible for human survival. Throughout the eighteenth century, disease was the greatest killer in European national navies, and scurvy was the greatest of the ship diseases, feared and dreaded like no other. With larger ships, longer voyages, and increased shipping traffic in that century, scurvy was a problem that was getting progressively worse— despite its already long and malignant pedigree that extended far back to the dawn of the Age of Sail.

SCURVY:
THE PLAGUE
OF THE SEA

IN THE BITTER WINTER OF 1535, a miserable
cluster of about one hundred French mariners
huddled about the drafty walls of a primitive pal-
isade fort in the woods along the shores of the frigid,
windswept St. Lawrence River. Within walking distance of their encampment was the Iroquois town of Stadacona
(near present-day Quebec City), a settlement of perhaps six hundred people. The three French ships had settled into the calm waters
of a nearby inlet and been frozen immobile the previous fall, just as
the northern winter tightened its grip upon the land. Bitter winds
tore in from the iced-over waterway, funnelled from the ocean hundreds of miles to the east. Although they were situated, according to
Jacques Cartier's calculation of latitude, farther south than St-Malo,
France, from which they had departed the year before, the winter,
the first New World winter ever experienced by any of them, proved
far harsher and longer than the men could have imagined. Ice glued
the ships in the waterway and three feet of snow smothered the
land. Without snowshoes and knowledge of the terrain, they were

paralyzed. Relations with the Natives were strained because Cartier had insulted them the previous summer by bypassing their settlement and sailing upriver to trade with their rivals at Hochelaga (Montreal).

Frightened, in a strange land, surrounded by unfamiliar and perhaps hostile people, and subsisting on aging rations purchased and stored in the ships' holds in France the year before, with only the occasional meal of fresh game obtained in trade from the Natives, the men soon were suffering from a mysterious malady. Nearly the entire crew was despondent and sickly. Their gums swelled hideously purple, and a horrid stench escaped from their gaping mouths. Listless and morose, too sick even to eat, they waited to die from the horrible plague that had descended upon them. After several weeks of suffering, the men began to die off.

The terrible scourge grew worse, until twenty-five of the "best and most able seamen we had" had succumbed to the disease and lay frozen and stiff, stacked like brittle cordwood in the holds of the ice-locked ships or stored in the compound of the primitive fort. Their shrunken faces, discoloured and grinning in the rictus of death, were a reminder to the living of the seemingly unavoidable destiny that awaited them. "We had," recorded Cartier, "almost lost hope of ever returning to France." Bewildered and frightened by their terrible predicament, and "because the disease was a strange one," Cartier ordered one of the men "opened, to see if anything could be found out about it, and the rest, if possible, cured." The disease that racked them was unlike any they had experienced before. The crude autopsy revealed a "white" and shrivelled heart surrounded by "more than a jugful of red date-coloured water." From the corpse's internal cavity issued "dark, tainted blood," while the lungs were "very black and gangrened." After the surgeon had done his work, unfortunately uncovering little practical information about the disease or its possible cure, the remaining men hastily buried their comrade as best they could in the frozen ground.

Cartier himself and two or three others, for some unknown reason, remained unaffected by the new plague, which they believed they had caught by coming in contact with several sickly Natives. "Our Captaine considering our estate (and how that sicknesse was encreased and hot amongst us) one day went foorth of the Forte," wrote the chronicler of the voyage, "and walking upon the yce, hee saw a troupe of those countrymen coming from Stadacona." Cartier was particularly curious to spy a man named Dom Agaya, who two weeks earlier had been nearly as sick as the Frenchmen, with "his knees swolne as bigge as a childe of two years old, all his sinews shrunk together, his teeth spoyled, his gummes rotten, and stinking." Cartier stared in astonishment at seeing him "whole and sound," and he was "marvellous glad" when Dom Agaya agreed to show him the cure for the mysterious malady. Cartier did not let on that virtually his entire crew lay ravaged by the terrible illness. Fearing that the Natives would observe their weakness and attack them, he convinced Dom Agaya that only one of his servants had contracted the disease.

Dom Agaya and two women from the village set off into the woods and returned with ten or twelve branches of a tree, probably the annedda (white cedar). The "juice and sappe" were apparently the remedy. Cartier and a few others who were still strong enough to rouse themselves followed Dom Agaya's instructions and boiled the bark and leaves in a great vat of water until it had become thick and the particles had settled. At first none of them would taste the ill-smelling brew, perhaps believing it to be poison, but "at length one or two thought they would risk a trial." The others watched curiously, knowing it was probably their only chance at survival. The brave few drank "the said decoction every other day, and put the dregs of it upon [their] legs that is sicke." So quick was the recovery of the mariners who had drunk the boiled broth that soon the sailors "were ready to kill one another" to get the miracle potion as fast as they could.

The Iroquois showing Jacques Cartier the secret of the annedda tree during Cartier's 1535 voyage to the St. Lawrence River. Without this knowledge of anti-scorbutics Cartier and all his men would have perished from the terrible ravages of scurvy.

Cartier and the few miraculously recovered men quickly went to the forest, where "a tree as big as any Oake in France was spoiled and lopped bare." They dragged the branches to the fort, skinned the bark off, and boiled it all into the turgid draft that would sustain their waning lives. The dying mariners greedily slurped it down. So astonishing was the recovery that within six days they had all regained their strength. "If all the phisicians of Montpelier and Lovaine had bene there with all the drugs of Alexandria," wrote an astonished Cartier, "they would not have done so much ine yere, as that tree did in six days, for so did it prevaile." They used the potion to remain healthy throughout the winter and then sailed home the next summer.

Like many of the European explorers at the dawn of the Age of Sail, Cartier had been searching for a source of easily plundered wealth or a route through North America to the Spice Islands. He was hoping to "discover certain islands and lands where it is said that a great quantity of gold and other precious things are to be found." This was a common goal of many sixteenth-century European voyages. After Columbus's trip across the Atlantic Ocean in 1492, Europeans began a centuries-long quest to explore the vast expanses of the world's oceans, inspired by the possibility of instant wealth and perhaps eager to escape the dejected squalor of their lives in the filthy, overcrowded, and disease-ridden cities of Europe. "Gold," exclaimed Columbus, "is a wonderful thing! Whoever owns it is lord of all he wants. With gold it is even possible to open for souls the way to paradise!"

Portuguese seafarers pioneered a commercial route around Africa, across the Indian Ocean to India, and then on to the Spice Islands, the Moluccas, in the distant east. Not only was spice valuable as a preservative of meats, or to mask the stench of rot on aging meat, but spices such as nutmeg and cloves were believed to be cures for various diseases that ravaged the European countryside. Certain spices were literally worth more than their weight in gold, and they proved a suitable inspiration for mariners to risk their lives sailing into the unknown. These early voyages were great leaps of faith equivalent to a modern expedition to Mars—premised on the faint hope of returning with fabulous wealth.

In the early sixteenth century, Spanish conquistadors such as Hernán Cortez and Francisco Pizarro brutally conquered and sub-jugated the Aztecs in Mexico, the Mayans in Central America, and the Incas in Peru. The quantities of silver and gold they plundered, or wrought from the earth with slave labour, were astronomical. Annual bullion fleets hauled this wealth back from Mexico and Peru, making Spain the richest European nation and inspiring Dutch, French, and English voyages of exploration, numerous privateers who waited along the shipping lanes, and later, colonial expansion. Throughout the sixteenth and seventeenth centuries, the mariners of these nations routinely plied the oceans of an ever-expanding world for exploration and trade. The mysterious disease that had plagued Cartier and his crew began to crop up more and more frequently.

Scurvy—*scorbuto, scarby, scorbu, skurvie, scorbuck*, or "the scor-butic taint"—turned up as a frightening ancillary to virtually every major voyage of discovery on record from Vasco da Gama, the Por-tuguese mariner who first sailed around the Cape of Good Hope in 1497 and established trade with India, to Francis Drake, the ruth-less English privateer of the Elizabethan era, to Cornelis Houtman, the brutal Dutch mariner who first led a trading voyage to the East Indies in 1595. John and Richard Hawkins, Samuel de Champlain, Vitus Bering, Pedro Cabral, Henry Hudson, Louis Antoine de Bougainville, John Davis, Willem Barents, and countless others—the list of recognizable names is long and exhaustive—similarly recorded the ravages of scurvy. The first naval commander to return from a long voyage and report that scurvy had not destroyed his crew was the celebrated Captain James Cook in 1770; he profited from a great effort by the British Admiralty to provide him with every known scurvy cure and a broad mandate to do whatever was needed to thwart the scourge. But the history of European naval exploration and expansion is the history of scurvy, and one looks in vain for a major expedition that did not suffer from it.

In 1519, the Portuguese mariner Ferdinand Magellan, hired by the Spanish king, departed Sanlúcar de Barrameda with three ships and 250 sailors to circumnavigate the globe and reach the Spice Islands by sailing west from South America rather than east around Africa. Only one ship and eighteen men survived the ordeal, limping into port three years later with a terrible tale of suffering and misadventure (Magellan himself was killed in the Philippines). Scurvy was the greatest killer, wiping out perhaps half of the crew in two major outbreaks, in the Pacific Ocean and the Indian Ocean, both when they were far from land and long at sea. A brief scan of the report of Antonio Pigafetta, an Italian mariner who kept a journal of the voyage, sheds some light on the conditions they endured: "They ate biscuit," he wrote, "and when there was no more of that they ate the crumbs, which were full of maggots and smelled strongly of mouse urine. They drank yellow water, already several days putrid. . . . Mice could be sold for half a ducat apiece, and still many who would have paid could not get them." But of all the horrible privations and suffering—a mariner's death by drowning, accident, or attack by natives was routine—the sea scurvy was singled out as the greatest horror of all. "Of all our misfortunes," wrote Pigafetta, "this was the worst: the gums of some of the men swelled over their upper and lower teeth, so that they could not eat and so died."

Although a distemper with similar symptoms had been known since the time of the ancient Greeks, and was reported by Roman legionaries when they marched in the lands of northern Europe, the ailment was soon associated with the sea and became known as the mariners' disease. Scurvy was first recorded at the dawn of the Age of Sail, in the late fifteenth century, and it immediately became a routine fact of life on all long-distance voyages and was known to all the European maritime nations. It was universally dreaded. Usually it struck when ships were far from home, near the coasts of distant lands—when sailors had been living on the food prepared and stored in their home ports for months on end. Shipowners and governments counted on a 50 percent death rate for sailors from scurvy on any major voyage.

The symptoms of the mariners' disease remained consistent. Skin became waxy and discoloured with black splotches, and clear thinking was impossible. Untreated, it led to a slow, agonizing, and inevitable death. One classic description from 1596 was recorded by the English sea surgeon William Clowes. "Their gums were rotten even to the very roots of their very teeth, and their cheeks hard and swollen, the teeth were loose neere ready to fall out . . . their breath a filthy savour. The legs were feeble and so weak, that they were not scarce able to carrie their bodies. Moreover they were full of aches and paines, with many blewish and reddish staines or spots, some broad and some small like flea-biting."

Another classic early account of the disease was recorded by an unknown surgeon on a sixteenth-century English voyage. "It rotted all my gums, which gave out a black and putrid blood. My thighs and lower legs were black and gangrenous, and I was forced to use my knife each day to cut into the flesh in order to release this black and foul blood. I also used my knife on my gums, which were livid and growing over my teeth. . . . When I had cut away this dead flesh and caused much black blood to flow, I rinsed my mouth and teeth with my urine, rubbing them very hard. . . . And the unfortunate thing was that I could not eat, desiring more to swallow than to chew. . . . Many of our people died of it every day, and we saw bodies thrown into the sea constantly, three or four at a time. For the most part they died without aid given them, expiring behind some case or chest, their eyes and the soles of their feet gnawed away by the rats."

Georg Steller, the naturalist who sailed with Vitus Bering to Alaska in 1741, described the horrors aboard the ship when scurvy had taken hold of nearly every mariner. "Not only did the sick die off," Steller reported, "but those who according to their own assertion were well, on being relieved at their posts, dropped dead from exhaustion. . . . The cold, dampness, nakedness, vermin, fright, and terror were not the least important causes. . . . The most eloquent pen would find itself too weak to describe our misery."

Luis de Camoens, a Portuguese poet and chronicler of da Gama's voyage, penned a verse to describe the sickness of the mariners, perhaps the first poem dedicated to scurvy. It probably loses something in translation:

The gums within the mouth swelled horribly
And all the flesh about it tumid grew,
And as it swelled apace, it rotted too.

Scurvy was everywhere—an ever-present arm of the Grim Reaper, clutching and grasping at mariners as they laboured on ships slowly plying the world's oceans, plucking at the thin strand that bound them to the world of the living. But scurvy did not always claim its victims. Truly remarkable—miraculous, some would claim—cures were recorded when the best medical opinion, and common sense, predicted no chance of recovery. Some patients, wretches who looked as if they had nearly melted away from the disease, were up and about, springing to their duties within a week of being written off—all traces of the disease seemingly vanished from their bodies. By comparison, someone ravaged by virtually any one of the other common diseases of the time—the plague, malaria, yellow fever, syphilis, measles—could never have recovered to full health once it had so thoroughly taken hold of him. There was no reliable explanation for how anyone could possibly rebound from an affliction that had basically eaten through his body, so it was, according to one early-eighteenth-century report, chalked up to "divine permission."

The wildest, most fanciful notions were put forward to explain scurvy, seemingly against all common sense. A French surgeon named Monsieur Lescarbot speculated in 1605 that the disease was caused by the "bad quality of the air . . . the great rottenness in the woods," and "an indigestion of rude, gross, cold and melencholy meats, which offend the stomache." It could be cured by eating "good sauces . . . good Capons, good Partridges, good Ducks, and good rabbits and . . . the young buds of herbs in the Spring be also very sovereign." Failing this, he advised "for every one to have the honest company of his lawfull wife: for without that, ones minde is always upon that which one loves and desireth; the body becomes full of ill-humours, and so the sickness doth breed." The French mariner François Pyrard, writing after a 1603 voyage to the East Indies, believed that the distemper was "very contagious even by approaching or breathing another's breath," while Thomas Cavendish, on a 1586 British circumnavigation of the globe, suggested that scurvy was "an infection of the blood and liver." Antonie Knivet recorded, on a 1591 voyage through the Straits of Magellan to explore the South Seas with John Davis, that "most of our men fell sicke of the Scurvie by reason of the extreme heat of the Sunne, and the vapours of the night." Bad air, exposure to sea water, heredity, contagion, rats, divine disfavour, dampness, overly salted food, a too hot climate, a too cold climate, laziness, the weakness of northern peoples—all were offered as causes of scurvy in the accounts of the early mariners.

In fact, despite the similar symptoms, no one could ever agree on what scurvy actually was, what caused it, and what might cure it. The disease occurred in stormy weather and in fine weather, under cloud and sun, close to land and in the middle of the ocean. Neither the cargo nor the nature of the ship's mission seemed to have an effect. Having a priest aboard brought no relief—except perhaps to the dying. To early mariners, there seemed to be only three common threads linking the innumerable reports of the disease: scurvy was associated with the sea and a naval life; it attacked northern peoples more than the southern ones they encountered, many of whom had never experienced the illness; and it occurred after several months at sea. Occasionally the idea that it might be caused by diet came into vogue, yet this line of reasoning was quickly subsumed under the waves of other, sometimes wildly off-base, proposals.

One theory that cropped up again and again over the centuries was a classic case of mistaking early symptoms of the problem for the root cause. The first signs of scurvy in a crew were lassitude and melancholy, and some early theorists believed that "laziness and sloth" were the direct cause of the later symptoms. Following this line of reasoning, they advocated increasing sailors' workloads, something that could have actually increased the spread of the disease by draining what little energy reserves remained among the mariners. The chronicler of Edward Fenton's 1582 voyage to the Pacific, for example, suggested that "the more exercise within reason the better, for if you for once fall to laziness and sloth, then the scarby is ready to catch you by the bones and will shake out every tooth in your head." As late as 1736, the physician and naval surgeon William Cockburn declared in his influential book *Sea Diseases* that scurvy had nothing to do with diet and everything to do with idleness, which hindered digestion, thereby causing scurvy. With greater physical exertion, he claimed, "digestion and nutrition were better performed," and scurvy could be held at bay. Another claim, by John White in 1712, suggested that fresh fruit was a direct cause of enteritis, inflammation of the small intestine, and that "one must, when ships reach countries abounding in oranges, lemons, pineapples etc., ensure that the crew eat very little of them since they are the commonest cause of fevers and obstruction of the vital organs."

Occasionally a person was cured by accident, as happened with the fortunate sailor treated by the English surgeon William Clowes in 1596. After bleeding him, Clowes fed the man a mug of ale fortified with pepper, cinnamon, ginger, saffron, watercress, and scurvy grass. "Thus," he claimed, the man was miraculously cured "by the help of God and careful diligence" and soon returned to active duty. Clowes doesn't mention whether he knew which were the active ingredients of this seemingly randomly created concoction (the watercress and scurvy grass, or spoonwort), nor is there any record of its having been tried again. Clowes might well have suspected the bloodletting was the beneficial treatment; certainly it remained in vogue as a scurvy treatment for two centuries thereafter.

Most of the common scurvy cures during the Age of Sail were, with hindsight and better knowledge, completely ineffective, yet people swore by them, entirely convinced of their efficacy. One sixteenth-century recipe calls for scurvy grass to be deep-fried with eggs in train oil (oil made from boiling seal carcasses and skimming the fatty scum from the surface of the pot). Richard Hawkins felt that it could be cured by "the air of the land; for the sea is natural for fishes, and the land for men." An aging English mariner named William Hutchinson wrote in 1794 of his own experience with scurvy half a century earlier. Even at that late date, Hutchinson believed that salty food had caused his scurvy, and that drinking a daily cup of tea had cured it. "It has been my custom," he wrote, "ever since, to drink tea, twice a day, when I could get it. And to let lovers of tea know, I have made it in a very nice manner on board a ship. . . . With the above proposed method of living, I kept clear of the scurvy during the rest of the voyage, when many of my ship mates died with it . . . [and] have, ever since enjoyed an uncommon share of health." At that time, there was no reliable information to back up medical opinions, nor was there any consensus amongst nations or even individuals on the causes of the mysterious malady.

When the European mariners came into contact with peoples from around the world, it seemed that no one else suffered from it.

In some accounts it is referred to as the European disease, and the Portuguese, Spanish, French, English, Dutch, and Russians were believed to be particularly susceptible to it—hardly surprising, considering those were the major maritime nations of the time. While Cartier recorded in 1535 that the Natives along the St. Lawrence had a cure for the ailment, later reports suggested that these peoples didn't routinely suffer from it. (Cartier was fortunate to have seen Dom Agaya while he was temporarily ill with symptoms similar to those of his sailors, and so to ask him for a cure.) Nor did Inuit in the Arctic suffer from it, despite following a diet devoid of fresh vegetables, milk, cheese, and grains—a diet, in fact, consisting exclusively of raw meat and fish for the majority of the year. Arabic desert dwellers of the Middle East also had no problems, leading early medical theorists away from blaming dietary deficiencies.

Nevertheless, from scurvy's earliest recorded occurrences at sea, ships' captains and surgeons from all European nations suspected that the standard sea rations, which were dried, heavily salted, and often rancid, were somehow to blame—they speculated that the poor food perhaps weakened the body, thereby allowing the disease to take hold. Numerous accounts report that after several days ashore, mariners saw their health improve dramatically. But anyone who had spent time at sea also knew that shipboard conditions and diet were exceedingly difficult to change—a healthy diet, clean water, and a dry sleeping space were impossible on long sea voyages. Early seafarers such as the Norse and the Chinese knew the value of taking fresh cranberries, seaweed, or ginger on ships, and this would have helped hold scurvy at bay for the shorter voyages undertaken by these nations. Mariners of the Dutch East India Company briefly tried to grow gardens on the decks of their ships in the seventeenth century, but the experiment failed because storms and rolling waves washed the soil away. Other European merchants likewise tried to include various easily accessible and cheap dietary supplements such as pickled and oiled vegetables, scurvy grass, watercress, or dried fruits on distant voyages, but while they might have been effective on smaller ships on shorter voyages, it became impossible with the increasing size of European ships and length of time at sea to provide enough fresh foods to stave off scurvy.

Although scurvy's cure seems obvious from a modern perspective, it remained the greatest medical mystery of the Age of Sail for good reason. The key element to a cure—ascorbic acid, or vitamin C— was effectively invisible to early surgeons, physicians, and scientists. Fruits and vegetables all have different quantities of ascorbic acid, and in the eighteenth century it was hard to imagine, and impossible to rationally theorize, why one would be loaded with ascorbic acid while another was devoid of it. Cucumbers, for example, have very little vitamin C, while broccoli is one of the most concentrated sources. Oranges and lemons contain nearly ten times the levels of the vitamin in apples and at least double the quantity in limes. Fresh raw liver and kidneys, prized food items in the Arctic and in the desert, contain significant quantities of the mysterious acid, while regular meats contain only marginal amounts—and dried, aged, or heavily cooked meat contains none at all. Potatoes have small quantities of the essential vitamin, while rosehips are loaded. Dried grains have no vitamin C, and neither do eggs or cheese, although yogurt contains a small amount. Wine, cider, and beer might contain limited quantities of the vitamin, depending on how they were made; stronger liquors contain none at all.

A tour of a modern supermarket reveals an array of foods and drinks that are "cures" for the disease. Shoppers can buy fruits and vegetables from around the globe, even in mid-winter, and many processed foods and drinks are also fortified with ascorbic acid. Refrigeration allows year-round access to fresh fruits and vegetables, even in northern countries with long winters. We can buy vitamin C in tablets and eat it any time we choose. Even a fast-food burger comes with fresh onions, lettuce, and tomatoes; though these provide only a minimal quantity of ascorbic acid, it is sufficient to ward off the more debilitating symptoms of scurvy. It would be very difficult for an individual to come down with scurvy in this day and age, but if someone did, the symptoms would be readily identified and the cure obvious and easily obtained, at very little cost.

The symptoms and the progression of the disease have been well and reliably outlined in a succession of medical texts. Modern science, however, more fully understands the degenerative process that results in scurvy's symptoms. Ascorbic acid is needed by humans to create and maintain an important enzyme known as prolyl hydroxylase. Without this enzyme, the body cannot manufacture the protein collagen, which is the binding material vital for maintaining internal connective tissue, bones, and dentin in teeth. When we are injured, collagen is the mortar that reconnects the torn tissues and broken bones. Defective collagen allows the walls of blood capillaries to come unglued, bone tissue to unravel, and the gums to disintegrate. Dentin, a substance at the root of our teeth, also degenerates without ascorbic acid, causing teeth to become loose and wobbly, and eventually to fall out. Scurvy is nothing less than the body's slowly falling apart, its internal components collapsing because they lack the glue to hold them together. Strangely, only guinea pigs and certain species of primates and bats share with humans the inability to internally manufacture ascorbic acid, which creates the enzyme that manufactures collagen. Most animals create their own ascorbic acid and can never fall prey to scurvy.

Ascorbic acid, its related enzyme, and its effect on humans are still not entirely understood. Linus Pauling, for example, the guru of vitamin C therapy in the 1970s and a pioneer of clinical studies involving ascorbic acid, was the most prominent of a group of researchers who recommend hyper-dosing on it as a cure for a seemingly incongruous collection of ailments. One of the controversial theories advanced by this group suggests that modern heart disease is the body's response to mild symptoms of scurvy, and that the scarring and plaque buildup in arteries commonly associated with heart disease are the body's attempts to patch up deteriorating internal vessels because of the deficiency of ascorbic acid. According to this theory, the buildup of cholesterol and plaque was a survival mechanism the human species developed during the ice ages— during times when the cold and inclement weather of long winters resulted in humans living for prolonged periods on diets deficient in the ascorbic acid found in fresh foods—and heart disease has, for the moment, outlived its genetic usefulness. These theories are speculative, however, and are not generally accepted within the medical or scientific communities.

The accepted clinical signs and symptoms of scurvy appear slowly, after about sixty to ninety days on a deficient diet (although scurvy regularly appeared on ships much sooner because sailors were deficient even before setting sail). Psychological signs such as melancholy, moroseness, listlessness, and lack of motivation precede physical manifestations such as weakness, lack of coordination, easy bruising, aching joints, and swelling in the extremities. Later the gums swell and become spongy and blood-soaked, breath becomes foul, and the skin becomes sallow and rubbery. Internal hemorrhaging causes purple splotches on the skin and under the eyes, and eventually, in the latter stages of the disease, once healed broken bones come apart. Without an infusion of ascorbic acid, the internal hemorrhaging near the heart and brain, usually after sudden exertion such as sitting up, causes death. Nothing else will reverse the ill effects.

The level of ascorbic acid in an average healthy body ranges between 900 and 1,500 milligrams. The human body uses about 50 milligrams of the vitamin daily, and the symptoms of scurvy begin to show themselves when the base level drops below 500 milligrams and progressively worsen the longer the body's reserves of ascorbic acid remain low. As people get older their ability to store ascorbic acid decreases, which explains why often ships' boys were the least affected by the ravages of scurvy and had greater survival rates. Different countries recommend different amounts of ascorbic acid as part of a daily diet. The World Health Organization recommends 30 milligrams, while the United States recommends 60 milligrams. (See the Appendix for a list of the quantities of ascorbic acid in a number of common foods.) Because the body continuously uses ascorbic acid, certain foods with low levels of vitamin C, such as sauerkraut, could have been an effective medium-term preventative on ships, but not an effective cure—when the body's supply of ascorbic acid is around or below 500 milligrams, merely replenishing the minimal amount consumed by the body each day will only slow down the degenerative process.

The best way to avoid scurvy is never to allow the body's ascorbic acid to drop below the normal level. Waiting for symptoms to appear before trying to "cure" the sickness, as was typically done on ships during the Age of Sail, will compound the problem immeasurably. Shipboard, this necessitated as a cure the use of foodstuffs with very high levels of ascorbic acid—the very foods that were virtually impossible to store and preserve aboard ship. If, instead, mariners had eaten sauerkraut every day of a long voyage, scurvy might have been held at bay for much longer than the standard sixty or so days. By the time symptoms appeared, however, it would have been physically impossible for a mariner to consume a quantity of the fermented cabbage sufficient to raise his body's ascorbic acid back to a healthy level.

The conditions under which common sailors lived and laboured also made them particularly susceptible to the ravages of scurvy. Life at sea was not conducive to maintaining good health. Modern research has confirmed that the body consumes increased quantities of ascorbic acid in cold, damp conditions, with erratic and insufficient sleep, and under extreme stress, such as the fear resulting from the threat of violent punishments, storms, or battle. The body also consumes increased quantities of ascorbic acid while fighting infection and fever, and when healing from wounds. Scurvy could not easily be prevented on ships because the conditions under which mariners laboured and lived were precisely what made the disease inevitable. Because of their lifestyle, mariners in the Age of Sail needed more vitamin C than the average landsmen, not less, just to hold scurvy at bay.

Compounding the problem was the health of the average seamen. When men willingly joined the navy, it was usually after a long winter when they had not eaten fresh foods for months. Prisoners languishing in jail had been eating poor foods and living in damp, wretched squalor before being sent to sea. A good number of the navy's pressed recruits, if not the vast majority, were showing the early signs of scurvy or other dietary deficiencies before they ever came aboard. Likewise, when crews were taken from incoming merchant ships, many of the men, after perhaps weeks or months at sea, were already feverish or on the verge of scurvy.

Even when captains knew that sailors were showing the early signs of scurvy, they were loath to put into port or to anchor close to shore to search for fresh provisions. In port desertion was a problem, while along coasts without friendly ports it could be dangerous business to send hunting parties and scavengers to search for greens. Unless the ship had a botanist on board (by the end of the eighteenth century, surgeons were encouraged to acquire this skill), captains had no way of identifying whether a plant was antiscorbutic, or indeed if it was poisonous. Because they could not be assured of finding relief for scurvy, a landing had little appeal. Putting into shore was also dangerous because of the likelihood of contracting fevers and dysentery. Even when a ship was anchored within close rowing distance of land, and even if the crew were showing the early signs of scurvy, officers would sometimes forbid sailors, apart from the water brigade, to go ashore—particularly in the sixteenth and seventeenth centuries, when so much of the world was new and unknown. By the eighteenth century landfalls were common and reasonably secure, but old prejudices lingered or military objectives allowed no time for a landfall. Scurvy at least was slow and predictable, but many of the other unknown ailments brought a quick death that spread indiscriminately throughout the entire ship, including even the captain. The famed naval captains Francis Drake and Richard Hawkins both succumbed to "a bloody fever" (probably yellow fever) in the West Indies in 1596. As already noted, officers tended to be less afflicted with scurvy than the crew, however, owing to their better health and diet, and would have been far more likely to choose the slow, selective ravages of scurvy over the quick, indiscriminate virulence of yellow fever or malaria.

Weakened by scurvy, mariners were more susceptible to other diseases, such as yellow fever, tuberculosis, or dysentery. Racked by diseases that weakened their constitutions, they were at increased likelihood for scurvy. Common sailors could not have avoided scurvy even when they ate a diet with enough ascorbic acid to have kept land dwellers free from the scourge, which is partly why a disease so simple from a modern perspective was so bewildering and mysterious in past centuries.

Complicating the issue further, and confounding the early surgeons and scientists who sought a cure at the time, is the inherent fragility of ascorbic acid. Merely cutting or bruising a vegetable or fruit can cause a significant loss of the vital acid, while processing it with heat, even for ordinary cooking, also causes a significant loss. If copper pots are used for cooking, as was standard on eighteenth-century naval ships, well over half, perhaps as much as 75 percent, of the ascorbic acid is destroyed. Cabbage boiled in a copper pot will lose more than two-thirds of its ascorbic acid, whereas an equivalent amount cooked in an iron pot will lose less than one-fifth. In 1757 the English sea surgeon John Travis erroneously proposed that scurvy was little other than copper poisoning caused by the verdigris in the "slush" that remained after cooking salt meat. Aging or drying foods also destroys at least half of the ascorbic acid, if not more (dried peas or beans, for example, have none). And the longer a food ages, the more ascorbic acid is lost. Because of this confusion, the discovery of a practical cure for scurvy was a major scientific breakthrough for its time, no less important than the discovery of the chemical structure of ascorbic acid and how to synthesize it 150 years later.

In the Age of Sail, however, nothing of ascorbic acid was known —nor could it have been known, as limited as early physicians and scientists were by their own stubborn theories and by technology too primitive for the task. But by the mid-1700s, the navies of western Europe were desperate for a cure—so great were the casualties of mariners at sea, and so great the political and commercial ramifications of allowing scurvy to run rampant. Scurvy was the demon of ocean-going travel. One voyage in particular revealed the horrendous costs of ignoring scurvy and mobilized the British Royal Navy and the medical establishment to begin the decades-long search for a practical solution to the plague of the seas.

3

DISASTER AND VICTORY
IN THE SOUTH SEAS:
LORD ANSON'S
TERRIBLE VOYAGE

ON MARCH 7, 1741, after weeks of fine sailing, an English squadron cruising around Cape Horn, the southern tip of South America, was buffeted by erratic gusts of wind from the south, the forerunner of a terrible storm. The sun was slowly enveloped in cloud and mist, the waves grew ponderous and dark, and the wind rose to a ferocious moan. The autumn gales of the southern hemisphere had begun. It was, according to the official chronicle of George Anson's expedition, "the last cheerful day that the greatest part of us would ever live to enjoy."

For the men of those five warships and one sloop, it was the beginning of a three-month battle for their lives. The ships struggled southwest against the incessant wind and surging currents that threatened to drag them back east onto the jagged, rock-bound coast. Winds tore at the rigging from erratic angles; purple-and-black clouds rolled across the sky, making navigation impossible;

and ragged froth was whipped across the deck. The ships pitched in the wild sea, water pouring in the hatches as they pounded into rising waves. For weeks the tempest raged, keeping them at sea far longer than they had planned. The ships were spun about uncontrollably, occasionally teetering on the precipice of the curling tongue of a "mountainous overgrown sea" before plunging into the heaving valleys between the waves, the timbers shuddering and groaning under the impact. "The fury of all the storms which we had hitherto encountered seemed to be combined," reads the chronicle of the voyage, "and to have conspired our destruction."

As the storms increased in severity beyond the wildest imaginings of the mariners, who were already enfeebled by dysentery and typhus, scurvy began to spread its ugly tendrils. Just when they needed their strength the most to battle the furious storm, they grew weaker by the day. The lower decks were awash with sickly bodily fluids, and men lay prostrate in the slime, sluicing about as the ships bucked and spun in the gale. Several of the oldest sailors were horrified when old battle wounds sustained decades earlier began to bleed anew and shattered leg bones separated again, causing bewilderment and excruciating pain. "This disease . . . so particularly destructive to us, is surely the most singular and unaccountable of any that affects the human body. For its symptoms are inconstant and innumerable, and its progress and effects extremely irregular." At first only a third of them lay ill, swaying in their hammocks in the reeking bowels of the ship. Soon their teeth became wobbly, their gums turned black, and they lost the will to man the ship. "Some lost their Senses, some had their sinews contracted in such a Manner as to draw their Limbs close to their Thyghs, and some rotted away."

Seldom did a day pass that a man did not expire in the dim, fetid hold where their hammocks were strung up. They perished with agony frozen on their ghastly countenances. The log of the largest warship, the *Centurion*, records death from scurvy as a routine entry, often several per day. April 18: "Richard Dolby and Robert Hood

Anson's ship off South America.

seamen and William Thompson marine deceased." April 28: "Robert Pierce, John Mell, seamen deceased." May 13: "Arthur James, Vernon Head seamen deceased. The latter died suddenly." Finally, after a month and a half of daily deaths, even their names were too much bother to write down in the ship's log. May 28: "Two more seamen died and three soldiers." Some of the dead men were sewn into their hammocks and pitched overboard, but as the disease progressed, the living mariners became too enfeebled to deal with the dead. Many were tumbled into the hold, where they stiffened and washed about, while others lay stranded on the deck, lurching from side to side with the motion of the ship. In the month of April, the *Centurion* lost forty-three men to scurvy, and in May, as the ship turned north and the men hoped that with milder weather, "its [scurvy's] malignity would abate," they lost perhaps twice that number. The squadron was blown about the wind-whipped ocean, with barely a handful of days of stable weather, until the end of May, when the storm finally eased and the skies momentarily cleared.

During the terrible ordeal two of the ships had abandoned all hope of pressing around the Horn and retreated to the Atlantic, while a third was in serious trouble. Containing a great number of invalids and fever-racked patients even before scurvy broke out, the *Wager* was further disabled when the storm snapped her mizzen mast, leaving her with a shattered stump incapable of holding much sail. As the ship picked its way north along the jagged and desolate west coast of Chile, storms continued to rattle her, scurvy took most of the men out of commission, and the ship was in danger of foundering. On the fourteenth of May 1741, the *Wager* struck the rocky coast and was torn asunder, with many perishing horribly because they were too weak to scramble ashore against the rumbling surf.

Commodore George Anson led a squadron of ships on a four-year voyage that historians have described as the worst medical disaster ever at sea. Most of Anson's crew were killed by scurvy; only one of the five warships that departed England in 1741 made it home.

In late 1739, England and Spain had declared war over trade and sovereignty rights in the Caribbean, and George Anson, an as-yet-undistinguished officer of middle years, who had fought as a young man against the Spanish at the Battle of Passaro in 1718 and had commanded ships in trade-protection duties off the coast of South Carolina and Guinea, was commissioned to lead a six-ship fleet to the South Seas, the Pacific coast of South America. His mission was bold and unprecedented for the Royal Navy. After arriving in the Pacific, he was instructed to "do your best to annoy and distress the Spaniards . . . by taking, sinking, burning, or otherwise destroying all their ships and vessels that you shall meet with." He was also commissioned to attack a few towns and, most important, to capture the Manila treasure galleon, the Spanish ship that hauled silver between Acapulco and the Philippines. Because of its immense value it was known as "the Prize of All the Oceans," and it had been captured twice before by English privateers (Thomas Cavendish in 1587 and Woodes Rogers in 1709), but never in an official Royal Navy operation. Anson's expedition was a dangerous and important military manoeuvre designed to strike at the heart of Spanish trade and commerce.

To accomplish this mission, Anson was given command of five two-decked ships of the line, one single-decked sloop, and two small supply vessels. Although Anson's fleet did not leave Spithead, England, until mid-September, it began assembling in February 1740. The warships consisted of the massive flagship *Centurion*, at 1,005 tons and 60 guns; the *Gloucester* and the *Severn*, each at 853 tons and 50 guns; the *Pearl* and the *Wager*, at 600 tons with 40 guns and 24 guns, respectively; and the 200-ton sloop *Tryal*. The ships needed repairs to the masts and sails, and reorganized cabins and lower decks to accommodate the increased number of sailors and marines required for the mission. For months the ships were delayed in the dockyards, which were already overcrowded as the navy hurriedly mobilized dozens of ships for the impending war.

Finding the thousands of able-bodied sailors and marines proved to be an even more daunting task than repairing the ships. While the dockyards were working around the clock renovating aging ships, and the victuallers were furiously busy trying to gather provisions, press gangs prowled the warrens of dockside towns for new recruits. But the overcrowding helped the spread of contagious diseases such as typhus and dysentery, and sickness was wreaking terrible havoc in the seaside towns. The navy's sick list was expanding faster than the press gangs could find or capture new recruits, so the tally of able-bodied mariners actually decreased throughout the summer of 1740. The shortage of manpower rendered about a third of the navy's ships useless. Malnutrition was rife in the spring of 1740 because of a particularly long and cruel winter, and the cost of fresh food was unusually high, further compounding the problem. Many of even the healthiest members of Anson's crew hadn't eaten fresh vegetables or fruits in significant quantities for months, perhaps not since the fall harvest. They were not healthy men, even the best of them.

Anson needed around two thousand sailors, and by July 1740, though most of the major repairs had been completed on the ships, he was still several hundred short. He was anxious to depart as soon as possible, in order to have time to clear Cape Horn before the storm season began in March. But finding additional sailors and obtaining the final supplies were a bureaucratic nightmare, and he must have despaired of ever sailing. By early August he still could not fill his ships, and the Admiralty decided to clear out the pensioners from Chelsea Hospital and make them available for the mission. These five hundred men were veterans of earlier wars who had been maimed or driven mad, or who were too infirm to be on active duty. Many of them were over sixty years old, some over seventy. Some were incapable of walking and were carried aboard the ships on stretchers, begging to be released back to the hospital but unable to return themselves. They were, according to Anson, the most "crazy and infirm" the hospital had to offer, and entirely unfit for active service.

Anson was appalled, referring to them as "the most decrepit and miserable objects . . . much fitter for an infirmary than for any military duty." Offended and disgusted, he later wrote in the official account of his voyage that "without seeing the face of an enemy, or in the least promoting the success of the enterprise they were engaged in, they would in all probability uselessly perish by lingering and painful diseases; and this too, after they had spent the activity and strength of their youth in their country's service." The Admiralty was attempting to clear out the hospitals before the war to make way for the anticipated new wounded who would soon be arriving; certainly the navy must have been aware that very few of the invalids would be fit for the rigours of sea. In fact, only half of the released men arrived at Anson's ships; most of those who could walk had fled certain death aboard the fleet for uncertain but probable death in the slums of Portsmouth. Some of the deserters later applied at the hospital to reinstate their pensions and were mercifully received back. By the time the ships had reached western Chile, within a year of sailing, virtually all of the pensioners on board had perished, the bulk of them during the scurvy epidemic as they battled the storms of the Horn, fulfilling Anson's dire prediction. Entirely useless to the mission, the "aged and diseased detachment" contributed to overcrowding on the ships at the start of the voyage, which in turn helped to spread other diseases that killed many able-bodied seamen.

Anson was further dismayed when he beheld the contingent of marines who arrived to bolster his ship's company. Nearly all of them were young, frightened raw recruits who were "useless by their ignorance of their duty," and who had not "been so far trained, as to be permitted to fire." The bulk of them were already sick with fever or dysentery and were soon clogging up the holds of the ships, deliriously sweating in misery in the dank depths. As it had with the invalids, scurvy latched on to the marines with particular virulence and killed most of them; by the time the squadron reached Juan Fernandez Island, over 80 percent of them had perished. Tellingly, the *Wager*, the ship that was driven aground on the coast of Chile, contained the greatest number of invalids and marines; they out-numbered the able-bodied crew by 50 percent.

By late August the invalids had been settled aboard, the vast quantity of provisions needed for so large a crew had been secured, and the most grievous deficiencies in the ships' structures had been repaired. The squadron was ready to sally forth on its dangerous mission. It must have been exciting news indeed to many of the men who for nearly half a year had been living aboard the stationary vessels, subsisting on ship's rations enlivened by the occasional treat of fresh potatoes, leeks, or cabbage. Unfortunately, unfavourable winds kept them tethered to port for several more weeks, and then, in early September, Anson was unexpectedly ordered to chaperone a huge convoy of merchant and transport ships bound for the West Indies and North America. It was a tedious and slow business as 152 lumbering vessels clustered around Anson's squadron and puttered west. By the time Anson's fleet veered south to Madeira, off the southwest coast of Portugal, winds had again turned against him. The two-week voyage took nearly six weeks, and he did not spy the island until the end of October. Already men were dying aboard the ships, though scurvy had not yet manifested itself.

Because the squadron had remained "in port" for months before actually sailing, the sailors on board were eating ship's rations nearly devoid of fresh vegetables and fruit. Being in port did not have the same meaning for the crew of an eighteenth-century warship as it does for a modern traveller. Warships in port were anchored a con-siderable distance offshore for weeks or even months at a time, while the crew remained on board. They would have had little access to fresh foods and might not have been granted shore leave, except to join a press gang hunting for new recruits. Furthermore, the cost of

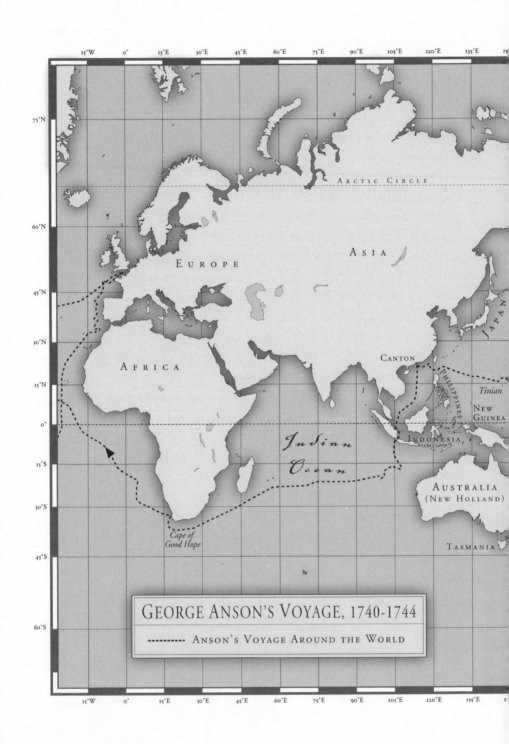

GEORGE ANSON'S VOYAGE, 1740-1744

---------- ANSON'S VOYAGE AROUND THE WORLD

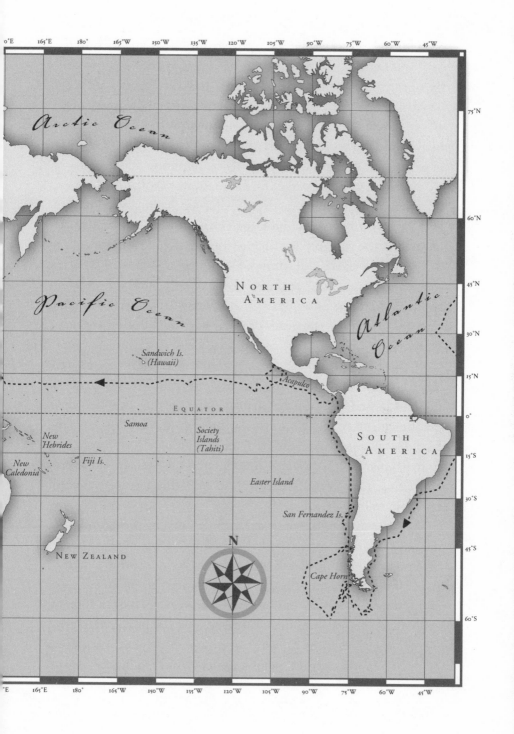

ARCTIC OCEAN

NORTH AMERICA

Pacific Ocean

Atlantic Ocean

Sandwich Is.
(Hawaii)

Acapulco

EQUATOR

Samoa

Society
Islands
(Tahiti)

New
Hebrides

Fiji Is.

New
Caledonia

SOUTH AMERICA

Easter Island

San Fernandez Is.

NEW ZEALAND

N

Cape Horn

food for so large a company was so expensive that quality suffered. So it was hardly surprising, and indeed Anson does not appear to have been much surprised, that disease, and particularly scurvy, had destroyed the vast bulk of his sailors, and hastened the wreck of the *Wager*, before he encountered a single Spanish ship. The Admiralty had ordered the standard antiscorbutic cures of the day: a daily draft of two ounces of vinegar, elixir of vitriol (sulphuric acid mixed with alcohol), and a potent patent medicine known as Ward's Drop and Pill (a viciously strong purgative and diuretic that many sailors took as the ships struggled around Cape Horn). Anson "gave a quantity of them to the surgeon, for such of the sick people as were willing to take them; several did so; though I know of none who believed they were of any service to them." Joshua Ward's quack medication contributed to the unsanitary squalor belowdecks, weakening the men and hastening the death of those who might otherwise have survived.

Because of the size of the expedition and the extraordinary length of time it took to organize and outfit it, French agents in London passed word to the Spanish, who hastily compiled their own squadron to chase Anson and prevent him from taking the fabulous treasure ship. Admiral Don José Pizarro led five warships from Santander in October 1740 to intercept Anson and thwart his ambitions. There would be two fleets of battleships chasing each other around the world.

Anson's squadron spent several months crossing the Atlantic and did not reach the coast of South America until December. Although they put into port on the island of St. Catherine's, off the coast of Brazil, for about a month, the men remained shipboard for most of this time. On St. Catherine's, "fruits and vegetables of all climates thrive here, almost without culture, and are to be procured in great plenty; so that here is no want of pine-apples, peaches, grapes, oranges, lemons, citrons, melons, apricots, nor plantains." Anson also purchased some onions and potatoes. But the produce was expensive because of the influence of the island's Portuguese governor, who placed "sentinels at all the avenues, to prevent the people from selling us any refreshments, except at such exorbitant rates as we could not afford to give." Anson and his pursers purchased only small quantities of these delicacies for the crew. Many of the sailors aboard ship, already sickly before coming aboard, had now gone at least six months with very little in the way of fresh foods that would have held scurvy at bay. Just as they were about to enter the most dangerous waters of the voyage, perhaps the most dangerous waters anywhere in the world—the notoriously fickle and turbulent passage round the Horn of South America—the crew were at their weakest and the seeds of scurvy began to germinate.

While Anson's ships ploughed around Cape Horn, heaving bodies overboard almost daily as they went, the Spanish squadron under Pizarro attempted to intercept them first at Madeira and then along the coast of South America. The Spanish fleet also attempted to round the Horn into the Pacific Ocean, rushing to be ahead of Anson and lie in wait off the western coast of South America. Pizarro's five ships had a gun total of 284, greater than Anson's six ships at 220. It was a formidable battle fleet that included the flagship *Asia*, of perhaps 1,200 tons and 66 guns; the *Guipuscoa*, of similar tonnage and 74 guns; the *Hermiona*, of around 850 to 900 tons and 54 guns; the *Esperanza*, of about 800 tons and 50 guns; and the *St. Estevan*, of about 600 tons and 40 guns. In total Pizarro commanded about 2,700 sailors; in addition, several hundred foot soldiers had been sent to reinforce garrisons in Peru. Although the Spanish ships were proportionately larger than the English ships, they too were extremely crowded for such a long voyage. They were also poorly provisioned. In their haste to catch up to Anson's fleet, they had rushed out of port in Spain provisioned for only four months, with instructions to obtain more food and water in Buenos Aires. Upon hearing a rumour that Anson lay in harbour at St. Catherine's, Pizarro rushed his ships from Buenos Aires before they were reprovisioned so he could try to sail around Cape Horn first.

The same storms that beset Anson's squadron in March 1741 also lashed the Spanish fleet, sucking the *Hermiona* and at least five hundred men beneath the waves in the terrible tempest. The *Guipuscoa*, carrying at least seven hundred men, was likewise battered by the storm and sent grinding into the rocky coast, killing half of them. The other three ships were violently sucked back east into the Atlantic and eventually rendezvoused at Montevideo, Uruguay, at the River Plata, in May, about the same time that the ruined remnants of Anson's squadron limped into Juan Fernandez Island. Pizarro's squadron had fared even worse. Not only did the mariners have no fresh foods, but they had been placed on starvation rations when the four-month supply of ship's provisions was depleted during their months-long battle with the storms of Cape Horn. There are no exact records of whether scurvy was rampant on the Spanish ships, but considering the time at sea and the lack of even standard rations, it is extremely unlikely that the Spanish sailors were eating anything fresh, and unlikely that scurvy could have been avoided under the circumstances. Undoubtedly, the weakened state of the mariners contributed to the loss of the two ships. Anson later wrote, after hearing a report of the Spanish commander's ordeal, that "they were reduced to such infinite distress, that rats, when they could be caught, were sold for four dollars a-piece." One sailor apparently concealed the death of his brother from the others for several days, sleeping in the hammock with the decaying corpse, in order to gain the man's meagre food allowance. More than half the crew on the three surviving ships were dead by the time they reached Montevideo.

The *St. Estevan* was too damaged to proceed, and the others, with split sails and snapped masts, could be only partially repaired during the summer. The following October, in 1741, the *Asia* and the *Esperanza* again attempted Cape Horn, but they were defeated and sent back a second time. Although Anson and the English fleet had no idea of the magnitude of the Spanish disaster in the spring of 1741, they had won their first victory, albeit not through any efforts of their own, but because the conditions and provisioning of the Spanish fleet were, against all probability, worse than their own.

After rounding Cape Horn, the remaining ships of Anson's convoy, scattered during the terrible months of storms, limped independently north towards their rendezvous on Juan Fernandez Island, a small island several hundred miles off the Chilean coast, directly west of Santiago. There they hoped to regroup and recuperate before pressing on with their mission. Men were dying of scurvy at a rate of five or six a day on the flagship alone, their bodies unceremoniously flung into the sea. The mortality rate was even higher on the other two vessels. Misfortune continued to plague them, and they did not arrive at the island until June, several weeks later than expected, because of an inability to accurately calculate their longitude and find their position at sea. As the *Centurion* sailed blindly about, searching for the island, about eighty more men succumbed to scurvy.

So many men had died from scurvy rounding Cape Horn that by the time the three ships anchored in Juan Fernandez Island, the *Centurion* had barely seventy men capable of duty. A second ship, the *Gloucester*, had "thrown overboard two-thirds of their complement, and of those that remained alive scarcely any were capable of doing duty, except the officers and their servants." And the smaller sloop *Tryal* likewise had buried more than half her complement, and only the captain, a lieutenant, and two sailors could "stand by the sails." The remaining mariners wept and stared in disbelief as they neared the distant outcropping of land. "It is scarcely credible with what eagerness and transport we viewed the shore, and with how much impatience we longed for the greens and other refreshments which were then in sight." Although the vessels were more wrecks than ships, with torn sails dangling from snapped masts and dying men crowding the decks for a glance at the long-sought land, the ships quietly floated into a harbour and dropped anchor as night crept upon them. Scarcely believing their deliverance, the few reasonably able-bodied men began ferrying ashore the sick and supplies, a task that consumed many days because of their weakened condition. Fortunately they were blessed with fair weather, because, as noted in the official report, "we could not, taking all our watches together, muster hands enough to work the ship in an emergency." Many of the mariners who hovered at death's door passed quietly away as soon as they were brought from the befouled interior of the ship into the clean air.

After establishing a makeshift encampment on the wooded and hilly island, they began tending to the sick and taking stock of the disaster. They were in the unknown waters adjacent to South America, officially at war with the people who inhabited the often bleak and inhospitable coasts. Although their orders called for them to boldly harass Spanish shipping, for many weeks they cowered in fear of even the smallest Spanish ship spying their encampment. They knew for certain that a Spanish battle squadron of five ships of the line had been dispatched to chase them into the Pacific, and if it spied them now, they would certainly be captured and probably killed. Although the English mariners still had two huge man-of-wars and a heavily armed sloop, there were not enough healthy men to sail a single ship into battle if the occasion arose. Anson, although a determined and optimistic man, knew that things did not look good. Somehow a naval force of great strength had been reduced to a bedraggled, tattered trio of badly damaged ships, with more than a thousand sailors already dead, mostly from scurvy, and hundreds more weak and limping about the shore scavenging for fresh foods. The prospect of completing their mission seemed dim as men continued to perish daily for more than a week after they landed.

Fortunately, Anson and the battered remnants of his expedition found Juan Fernandez Island to be a virtual paradise where grew "almost all the vegetables esteemed for the cure of scorbutic disorders. . . . These vegetables with the fish and the flesh we found here, were most salutary for recovering our sick, and of no mean service to us who were well, in destroying the lurking seeds of scurvy and in restoring us to our wonted strength." Some of the mariners reputedly shuddered and convulsed when they sank their wobbly teeth into the juicy fruit. After several months of painfully and slowly nursing themselves back to health, the remaining English sailors had recovered from their horrible ordeal and prepared to leave their island haven. But the death toll was astounding: of the approximately twelve hundred men who would have been on the three ships, only 335 remained alive. The normal ship's complement for the *Centurion* alone was around five hundred, and although enough sailors remained to sail all three ships, there were not enough to both sail them and man the great guns—each of these guns had a barrel around ten feet long, weighed about two tons, and needed a crew of six to ten men to operate. The *Centurion* was a sixty-gun ship, and the *Gloucester* was nearly as large.

In mid-September a sail was spied on the horizon. For months they had been expecting discovery by the Spaniards, either by Pizarro's fleet or by a patrol out of Peru, and it was only good fortune that had preserved them thus far. A makeshift crew was hastily assembled and loaded aboard the *Centurion*, which sallied forth to take it. It proved to be a lightly armed Spanish merchant ship voyaging from Lima, Peru, to Santiago, and it was taken without resistance after a few shots were fired over its bow. From the passengers, Anson learned the frightening news that a Spanish man-of-war had indeed been waiting for them at Juan Fernandez Island, but it had departed only days before they had arrived, believing them to have been destroyed rounding Cape Horn. Oddly, Anson's miscalculation of longitude, which had delayed the *Centurion* from landing at the island for nearly two weeks and cost the lives of perhaps eighty men, may have saved the entire squadron from capture and possibly death. Anson also learned of the terrible fate of Pizarro's fleet, the information having crossed the continent by land. He sent aboard some crew to command the captured ship and distributed the Spanish sailors amongst his ships to help sail them. During the next few months, they took several other Spanish merchant ships and stormed the small Spanish town of Paita, Peru, burning most of it to the ground. Then they sailed north to Acapulco, Mexico, searching for the Manila galleon, but they failed to encounter it. During all this time the men remained healthy and free from scurvy, probably because they frequently ate fresh provisions captured from merchant ships and plundered from shore. Before Spanish authorities could mobilize a fleet to track him down, and because merchant ships were now becoming wary after hearing news of his attacks, Anson decided to leave the Pacific coast of Spanish America. He ordered the release of the Spanish prisoners but kept the West Indians and Pacific Islanders to bolster his meagre crew.

Anson planned to spend two months crossing the Pacific to Canton, China, where the East India Company had a trading outpost. He ordered all the captured ships burned and scuttled; there were only men enough to provide a crew for the *Centurion* and the *Gloucester*. The prisoners were released near Acapulco, and the two ships, loaded with silver, gold, precious gems, and other valuable goods, headed west on May 6, 1742, late by several months for catching prime trade winds. Not surprisingly, they became becalmed, and during the dreadfully slow passage, scurvy again surfaced on the floundering ships. The surgeon and men alike were baffled because they had been drinking good water and eating reasonably good food; the ships were also clean and uncrowded, and fresh fish were frequently caught. The ships' logs make no mention of fresh fruits and vegetables, however. The first death occurred in the middle of the vast expanse of the Pacific Ocean on July 5, and deaths continued at the rate of about five per day. Ward's Drop and Pill needlessly weakened many of the men, and the vinegar and oil of vitriol were of course worthless.

The deaths from scurvy were as hideous and demoralizing as any ever recorded, and in mid-August Anson ordered the *Gloucester* abandoned because there were not enough men to repair the damaged masts and rigging. Of the *Gloucester*'s remaining ninety-seven men, only twenty-seven, including eleven young boys, could still stand on deck. The scurvy-ridden mariners were hoisted from the lower decks in nets and transferred to the ship's small boat, while the others broke into the liquor cabin and drank themselves silly before torching the ship. The hulk burned all night and then exploded at about 6 a.m., when the flames reached the powder magazine. "Thus ended the *Gloucester*," wrote one of the warrant officers, "a ship justly esteemed the beauty of the English navy." Aboard the *Centurion*, the sole remaining ship, the wretched crew continued to drop off "like rotten sheep" at the rate of ten per day. The ship was heavily laden with all the captured goods and had sprung a leak, but the crew were too weak to both sail the ship and repair the damage. Anson himself, once the aloof commodore of a proud fleet, now laboured at the pumps alongside the few able-bodied men who remained. Although the ship's log showed that they had sailed more than sixty-five hundred miles west from Acapulco, land was still nowhere in sight.

It was not until the end of August that the mariners spied the island of Tinian, in the Marianas chain. "I really believe," wrote Philip Saumarez, a lieutenant aboard the *Centurion*, that "had we stayed ten days longer at sea we should have lost the ship for want of men to navigate her." When the crippled ship put in to harbour, Anson personally helped row the dying ashore. The able-bodied cut open juicy oranges and squeezed the life-saving juice into the ruined mouths of the dying sailors. Tinian offered "cattle, hogs, lemons and oranges, which was the only treasure which we then wanted." It was not until the end of October that the men had recovered and the ship was reasonably repaired. Only a few hundred remained alive. Lieutenant Saumarez offered his own unprofessional opinion that scurvy "expresses itself in such dreadful symptoms as are scarce credible. . . . Nor can all the physicians, with all their *materia medica,* find a remedy for it." Nothing, he claimed, was "equal to the smell of a turf of grass or a dish of greens." Before leaving the island, Anson ordered the hold of the ship stuffed with oranges.

The bruised ship was barely seaworthy and limped into port at Macao, near Canton. After an interminable delay and much bureaucratic annoyance, Anson was able to secure help and supplies to properly repair the *Centurion.* In April 1743, he departed, still determined after all the hardships and danger, to attack the Manila galleon. With only 227 sailors on the *Centurion,* including several dozen young boys and some Dutch and Lascar seamen taken aboard at Macao, it was a foolhardy gamble. "All of us had the strongest apprehensions (and those not ill-founded)," wrote Anson, "either of dying of the scurvy, or of perishing with the ship, which, for want of hands to work her pumps, might in short time be expected to founder." Yet on the twentieth of June, 1743, in an unspectacular battle where the galleon struck her colours after ninety minutes, Anson took the *Covadonga,* the "Prize of all the Oceans," just off Cape Espíritu Santo in the Philippines. Only three of his men were killed in the battle and seventeen wounded, while sixty-seven were killed aboard the *Covadonga* and eighty-seven wounded. Although the *Covadonga* was a larger ship than the *Centurion,* and had a far larger crew, she was not a warship and her sailors were not warriors.

A

VOYAGE ROUND THE WORLD,

IN THE YEARS 1740, 41, 42, 43, 44.

BY GEORGE ANSON, Esq.

Commander-in-Chief of a Squadron of His Majesty's Ships, sent upon an Expedition to
the South Seas.

The "Centurion" taking the Spanish Galleon.

TO WHICH ARE PREFIXED,

A MEMOIR OF LORD ANSON, AND PREFACE.

LONDON:
INGRAM, COOKE, AND CO. 227, STRAND.
1853.

The title page to Anson's *A Voyage Round the World* showing the smaller
Centurion blasting away at the Spanish treasure galleon *Covadonga*. Despite
a sickly and short-handed crew, Anson was victorious and he and several
hundred survivors became fabulously rich.

Anson sailed both ships back to Macao, where the prisoners were discharged and the empty galleon sold.

The total haul from the exploit was tremendous, and when Anson and his remaining men returned to England, they paraded through the streets of London, in thirty-two heavily laden wagons, two to three million pounds of bullion. Anson's feat was the one shining success in a war that had seen few actions worthy of celebration. It was praised as a great victory despite the horrendous loss of life. Not only did the few hundred survivors become inordinately rich, but Anson, who received the lion's share of the booty, became fabulously wealthy and his reputation was made. He was quickly promoted to Admiral of the Blue and, in 1751, First Lord of the Admiralty, a position he held until his death in 1762, and through which he tried to introduce progressive changes to shipboard hygiene and encourage scurvy research. Only after the jubilation faded did the sobering reality of the number of lives lost temper the wild celebrations. No more than a few hundred of the two thousand men who had departed four years earlier survived. Of those who did survive, many were maimed, and the officers in particular claimed to have never regained their health entirely.

The end result of Anson's voyage, other than the usual riches and boost to national pride, was the beginning of a golden age of scurvy research in England. The voyage raised public awareness of the social cost of scurvy—everyone now knew that more British sailors routinely died from scurvy than from shipwreck, storms, all other diseases, and enemy action combined. Furthermore, ships like the *Gloucester*, which Anson was forced to abandon in the Pacific when scurvy had killed so many of his men, were outrageously expensive. It was becoming apparent that even if the Admiralty placed little value on the lives of the sailors, it did place value on its ships. When too many men died too quickly far from home waters, valuable ships had to be abandoned. No matter how grand a ship was, it was useless without sailors and marines to properly sail it.

Throughout the eighteenth century the danger posed by the wars with the French, the Seven Years' War, the War of American Independence, the French Revolution, and later Napoleon presented the greatest threat to England since the Spanish Armada two centuries earlier. Liberating the Royal Navy from the hobbling dominion of scurvy was paramount for national security. In the decades following Anson's voyage, there were perhaps a dozen different physicians who wrote about the disease and its cure. This compared to the handful of new ideas offered up in the previous two centuries. Despite the growing fashion for research into naval diseases, however, scurvy remained as great a mystery as ever for decades after Anson's voyage. Unravelling the intertwined threads of the scurvy problem meant tackling the very foundation of medical reasoning, for it in itself was a serious impediment to the advancement of new ideas, unsuited as it was to the problems and ailments of the new age being ushered in by the Industrial Revolution.

4

FOUND AND LOST: THE SEARCH FOR A CURE BEGINS

IN 1601 SIR JAMES LANCASTER, one of Elizabethan England's legendary bravos, a sea dog known for bold commercial undertakings and his battles against the Spanish Armada thirteen years earlier, was commissioned by the newly formed East India Company to lead a flotilla of four merchant ships on a pioneering voyage to the Spice Islands of the distant east. It was a dangerous but potentially profitable undertaking, ideally suited to a man of Lancaster's character. He would have been well aware of the greatest danger on such a voyage—danger that came not from shipwreck along one of the numerous uncharted shores or attack from rival, Portuguese merchants, but from scurvy and other diseases. He would have known, even at that early date, that a great number of his men—about half, judging from previous voyages—would perish miserably before the ships ever reached Sumatra or any of the other islands known to barter in spices. Lancaster's contemporary Sir Richard Hawkins wrote in the 1590s that "in twenty years, since I have been using the sea, I dare take upon me to give account of ten thousand men consumed with this disease."

The most surprising development of Lancaster's expedition, other than the fabulous wealth obtained from the cargo and trade contacts with which he eventually returned to England, was that he prevented scurvy from latching on to the crew of his flagship, the *Red Dragon* (although many of the men later perished from other diseases). While the crews of the other three vessels began to succumb to the dreaded disease as they rounded the southern tip of Africa, the men of the *Red Dragon* remained healthy and robust. "And the reason," wrote the chronicler of the voyage, "why the general's men stood in better health than the men of other ships was this: he [Lancaster] brought to sea with him certain bottles of the juice of lemons, which he gave to each one, as long as it would last, three spoonfuls every morning, fasting; not suffering them to eat anything after it till noon. . . . By this means the general cured many of his men and preserved the rest." Later in the voyage, when scurvy again surfaced, Lancaster led his ships into a port "to refresh our men with oranges and lemons, to clear ourselves of this disease." After purchasing thousands of lemons, he put his men to work squeezing them to make barrels of "lemon water," which was presumably the juice of lemons diluted with water.

For years English merchant ships used lemon juice regularly on long voyages, not only as a scurvy cure but, most significantly, as a preventative. In 1617 John Woodall, the surgeon general of the East India Company, wrote in *The Surgeon's Mate*, his medical treatise of advice and instructions to naval surgeons, that lemon juice was often used as a daily preventative on company ships. "There is a good quantity of juice of lemons sent in each ship out of England by the care of the merchants," he wrote, "and intended only for the relief of every poor man in his need, which is an admirable comfort to poor men in that disease." Merchant ships of the Dutch East India Company also made frequent use of lemon juice on their voyages. The Dutch company even maintained citrus plantations at key stops along the route, such as at Mauritius and the Cape of Good Hope. In the early 1600s scurvy was primarily a problem of merchant fleets, since national navies focused on coastal defence and were seldom stationed at, and infrequently sailed to, distant shores.

By the early years of the seventeenth century, lemon juice was well regarded as the universal solution to the scurvy problem. Although no one could explain why lemon juice was so effective, countless expeditions refer to its use both as a preventative and as a cure—though this good advice was often blended with other preposterous suggestions. François Pyrard sailed with two French ships to the Spice Islands in 1602 and recorded the inevitable attack of scurvy upon the mariners. In his detailed description of the distemper (including a grisly account of an autopsy that revealed shrunken, withered lungs and a swollen and blackened liver and brain), he observed that "there is no better or more certain cure than citrons and oranges and their juice: and after using it once successfully everyone makes provision of it to serve him when in need." Similarly, scurvy was known by early American colonists to be cured by lemon juice. Baron De La Warr, a governor of the colony at Plymouth in the early seventeenth century, sailed for the Caribbean when he came down with scurvy. "There I found help for my health," he wrote, "by means of fresh diet, and especially of oranges and lemons . . . an undoubted remedy for that disease."

How Lancaster knew about the benefits of lemon juice is a mystery. Perhaps it was because of his Portuguese upbringing. As a youth he lived for many years in Portugal to learn what was then the language of international trade. Perhaps it was there, where citrus fruits grew naturally and were a common and daily part of the diet, that he was privy to the wisdom of Portuguese merchants, who had been inadvertently curing scurvy on shorter voyages with lemon juice for decades. As early as the mid-sixteenth century, when the Portuguese were beginning to expand their trading empire east to India, Malaysia, and the Moluccas, the chronicler of a voyage led by Pedro Cabral recorded that when the *amalati de la boccha* (the curse of the mouth) had stricken many of the crew, the ships put into port in Mombasa, where they purchased fresh meat and fruit for their relief. The oranges, "the best in the world . . . made them well again." A late-sixteenth-century medical tract by the Mexican physician Augustin Faran advised that "to those who are careless, their gums are eaten away, their teeth are uncovered and their mouths are swollen. To stop this, they do the following: they take the juice of one half of a lime or sour orange and mix it with roasted or crushed alum."

Several early English privateers of the Elizabethan era were also aware of the curative properties of lemon juice. In the 1580s, Sir John Davis plundered potatoes and other fresh vegetables and fruits from Spanish habitations in South America and wrote of the benefits of fresh fruit against scurvy. And in the 1590s, Richard Hawkins traded for oranges and lemons with the Portuguese settlements in Brazil. "There was great joy amongst my company," he wrote, "and many, with the sight of the oranges and lemons, seemed to recover heart. This is a wonderful secret of the power and wisdom of God, that hath hidden so great and unknown virtue in this fruit, to be a certain remedy for this infirmity." Francis Drake also wrote that scurvy in his crew was cured by "plenty of lemons, which gave us good refreshing."

In the early years of the seventeenth century, the East India Company and the Dutch East India Company were able to keep scurvy at bay on many of their trading expeditions. But as the century progressed, scurvy reappeared as a mysterious and significant killer of crews. Somehow, lemon juice, or "lemon water," faded as the known and trusted remedy. Sea captains, still aware of the need for fresh produce, organized their voyages as a series of desperate dashes between foreign ports, instead of carrying bottles of "lemon water" with them. Unpredictable delays, ill winds, or bungled navigation resulted in terrible suffering and the loss of countless lives. The directors of the English and Dutch companies became complacent after years of effective prevention, and as the incidence of scurvy declined a new generation of corporate directors and sea captains began to question the value of expensive lemon juice—they might have thought they were paying handsome sums to greedy lemon merchants who revived the "myth" of scurvy to drive up the cost of a cure that was little other than a hoax. The sailors themselves complained about having to drink the bitter juice, as it was foreign to their northern palates, and the inconsistent quality and quantity issued to the sailors made it unreliable. By the 1630s, merely three decades after Lancaster successfully prevented an outbreak of scurvy on his pioneer voyage to the East Indies by issuing a small daily ration of lemon juice to each sailor, the East India Company was avidly pursuing tamarinds and oil of vitriol as the best antiscorbutic remedies.

The concept of preventative medicine also appears to have fallen out of favour. The thought of spending money to treat a disease that had not yet appeared in the crew was as foreign to seventeenth-century merchants as it later was to the national navies of England and France. Although lemon juice was sometimes carried aboard ships, it was usually kept in small quantities under the direct control of the surgeon and was to be used as a "cure" when scurvy appeared. But the problem of reserving lemon juice was that the quantities issued to the sick sailors were invariably too small. By the time symptoms of scurvy appeared, much greater amounts of ascorbic acid were needed to halt the inevitable decline and death. For a sailor who exhibited the classic symptoms, a spoonful of lemon juice would have had little beneficial effect, perhaps leading surgeons and captains to discredit it further.

There is no doubt that lemon juice was expensive. Lemons were not always in season and hence not always available on short notice to passing ships; English and Dutch ships would frequently have difficulty obtaining citrus fruits because for the most part they grew in Spain and Spanish-allied territories in the Mediterranean and east Atlantic. Catholic Spain was often at odds with Protestant England and Holland, and consequently the merchants of these countries sought out local cures that were more readily available or cheaper, such as sauerkraut or cider. In later editions of *The Surgeon's Mate*, John Woodall suggested scurvy grass, watercress, currants, gooseberries, turnips, radishes, nettles, and other plants as alternative, and more easily obtainable, antiscorbutics. Many of these plants were quite good sources of ascorbic acid when fresh. Dried, however, as they would have to have been to survive long ocean voyages, their effectiveness was greatly reduced, if not entirely eliminated.

In the 1660s, the Leipzig scientist Andreas Moellenbrok wrote favourably on the properties of dried spoonwort, and his praise of the "volatile salt of scurvygrass" led Dutch ships to be outfitted with water-distilling apparatuses for infusing the dried herb—to make a sort of scurvy-grass tea for the mariners at the first signs of the distemper. But dried scurvy grass had lost most of its ascorbic acid and had little positive effect on the mariners.

Scurvy also crippled Spanish and Portuguese ships, despite a reliable and cheaper supply of citrus fruits. On the ships of the Spanish Armada invading England in 1588, scurvy and other diseases were widespread. Disease was a significant, if underappreciated, aspect of the Armada's eventual defeat. Spanish and Portuguese physicians seem to have followed the same ill-fated path away from lemon juice as the English and the Dutch, and by the eighteenth century lemon juice was no longer standard issue on merchant ships. An early-eighteenth-century Spanish medical treatise by Father Juan de Esteyneffer claimed that scurvy "originates in obstructions of the liver and more often of the spleen. Also it is found in many organs or in abundance of the melancholic humors." For a cure he advocated a boiled herb broth that would have been of little benefit (although he added that lemon juice could be rubbed on afflicted gums).

As the length of voyages increased, scurvy became a greater problem than ever before. In certain years the death toll rose to over half the men who shipped out, and when shipwreck, sea battles, and the innumerable diseases of the Indies were added in, signing on as a sailor was a dangerous gamble. By the eighteenth century, it was not only merchant ships that were at sea for extensive periods of time but national navies as well—and by then the use of lemon juice as a cure was all but forgotten.

At the end of the seventeenth century, the notion that scurvy was caused by foul vapours or an imbalance in the bodily humours had replaced the practical, commonsensical observations of seamen, much to the detriment of mariners. Outlandish "cures" were the standard prescription of physicians and surgeons, and none would have had any beneficial effect on the suffering sailors. Strangely, these cures, preposterous by modern standards and useless in treating scurvy or almost any other sickness, had strong theoretical foundations and made perfect sense to the physicians of the era. The gradual decline in practical knowledge of antiscorbutics was matched by a rise in medical theorizing that sought to explain the sickness in terms of the basic principles of medicine as it was then understood.

The foundation of European medical theory at this time, and the basis from which diagnoses were made and cures derived, was the Hippocratic notion of achieving a proper balance between the four humours of the body. According to Hippocrates, "The body of man has in itself blood, phlegm, yellow bile, and black bile; these make up the nature of his body, and through these he feels pain or enjoys health. Now he enjoys the most perfect health when these elements are duly proportioned to one another in respect of compounding power and bulk, and when they are perfectly mingled. Pain is felt when one of these elements is in defect or excess, or is isolated in the body without being compounded in the body with all the others." It was believed that the humours were directly associated with distinct emotional states: the blood of the heart was associated with sanguinity, or a cheerful, optimistic disposition; the phlegm of the brain was associated with a calm, unemotional disposition; the yellow bile of the liver was linked to an easily angered or irritable character; and the black bile of the spleen was believed to be associated with melancholy or a gloomy and pensive disposition. The humours were believed to produce identifiable symptoms when out of balance. Therefore, to call someone "yellow" or "lily-livered" suggested that an excessive quantity of yellow bile was producing a feeble or cowardly disposition without anger, while someone exhibiting a melancholy temperament had an imbalance in his black bile and could be suffering from a scurvy—regardless of his diet or living conditions or proximity to other sufferers.

This foundation of medical theory had been handed down from the ancient Greeks and Romans centuries before, and it revived as Europe emerged from the Dark Ages. While modern science generally identifies the most recent studies as the most reliable, in the eighteenth century the opposite was true. The belief that humankind had been degenerating ever since being flung from the Garden of Eden meant that the older a scientific theory, the greater its credibility, because it had been produced by purer thinkers. Once the custom became entrenched, it was very difficult to change prevailing ideas. To understand the causes of and unearth potential cures for a sickness or disease, physicians and academics throughout Europe scoured the medical treatises of the ancient Greeks and Romans for ailments with similar symptoms. For example, the Cambridge nutritionist K. J. Carpenter, in his comprehensive book *The History of Scurvy and Vitamin C*, gives a detailed explanation of how the sixteenth-century Dutch physician John Echth came to his medical conclusions on scurvy. Echth boldly proclaimed, in *De Scorbuto*, that "scurvy is a disease of the spleen." Carpenter observes that "if this had been a modern work, one would at once assume that the statement had been based on autopsies in which the author had seen that the spleen looked grossly abnormal and/or that microscopic examination showed cellular changes. This is not what Echth had done."

To conduct his research, Echth combed ancient medical texts from thousands of years in the past, paying special attention to the oldest available. Scurvy, he postulated, most closely resembled illnesses described by the Greek geographer and historian Strabo in the first century B.C., and by the Roman theorist Pliny the Elder in the first century A.D. Strabo described the "stomakake" and "sceletyrbe" that was suffered by a Roman army in Egypt. The symptoms were "a kind of paralysis round the mouth and the latter round the legs, both being a result of the native water and herbs." Pliny wrote of a Roman army camped in Germany that suffered from an affliction that caused "loss of the teeth and total relaxation of the joints of the knees." Since these descriptions appeared to match the accepted symptoms of scurvy, Echth looked for similar descriptions in other writings, such as those of Celsus, from around 30 A.D., who wrote in *De Medicina* that "these in whom that spleens are enlarged, in these the gums are diseased, the mouth foul, or blood bursts out from some part. When none of these things happen, of necessity bad ulcers will be produced on the legs, and from these black scars." Thus Echth concluded that the putrid breath and stench of corruption, and the dark blotches that were the most common outward symptoms of early scurvy, meshed with this association with enlarged and blocked spleens (similar to the proposals of the Spanish physician Father Juan de Esteyneffer). With a blocked or swollen spleen, one of the four bodily humours, the black bile, could not be properly cleansed and disposed. Having its natural outlet from the body impeded, the black bile formed ulcers and dark splotches on the skin—the symptoms of scurvy. The corrupted blood was theoretically sluggish and also caused the weakness and lack of energy that were noted symptoms. Scurvy, it was concluded, was a universal disorder that had nothing to do with diet and everything to do with a blocked spleen. According to Severinus Euglenus, a respected seventeenth-century Dutch physician, scurvy was a "Proteus-like mischief, lurking under various and surprising appearances" and sent "by divine permission as a chastisement for the sins of the world."

Since scurvy was considered a problem of the black bile of the spleen, it needed to be treated with medicine that remedied the imbalance. Each of the four humours was believed to have a distinctive quality—blood was hot and wet, phlegm was cold and wet, yellow bile was hot and dry, and black bile was cold and dry. Since scurvy was a cold and dry sickness, it was to be cured with hot and wet medicines. Unfortunately, this theory often failed to mesh with reality. One of the only useful cures for scurvy, citrus juice, was classified as a "cold" medicine, and therefore deemed to be of no use. Oil of vitriol was likewise classified as a "cold" medicine, but it was routinely prescribed, even though it was actually of no benefit.

Physicians performed great philosophical back-flips and other mental acrobatics in a vain effort to reconcile common sense with their theoretical constructs. The respected Dutch physician Hermann Boerhaave, who taught at the University of Leiden and influenced the study of medicine across Europe, particularly at the University of Edinburgh (whence hailed virtually all Royal Navy physicians in the 1700s), so successfully advanced his personal version of the humoral concept that it permeated the education of nearly all European physicians in the early eighteenth century. Boerhaave proposed that there were two distinct types of "scorbutic taint," each with different causes and, therefore, different cures. A greatly simplified summary of Boerhaave's theory is that when the body's digestive system malfunctions, the partially digested foods trapped within the bowels become either acid or alkaline ("putrid"), depending on the food eaten. Ulcers such as those found in advanced scurvy were considered "acid acrimony," while the foul breath and rotting gums also associated with the disease were more akin to "alkaline acrimony." The dual components of scurvy—acid and alkaline—needed different treatment. Acid scurvy was said to be caused by an overly thin and acid blood serum, while the "other part" of the blood was too thick. Boerhaave's solution was of no practical value, except that by accident citrus juice was classified, along with vinegar, sulphuric acid, and Moselle wine, as useful for boosting the acidity of the blood and thinning its excessive alkalinity. Alkaline, or "putrid," scurvy needed a warm cure such as ginger or volatile salts. Other physicians proposed variations on this model. For example, some suggested that acid scurvy was a hot condition that needed an alkaline cure such as blood-letting (the passionate heat of the blood would be rebalanced by draining it, eliminating a hot-blooded temperament).

Boerhaave also believed that the originating imbalance that led to all diseases was caused by foul vapours that created internal blockages; thus all cures were linked to air quality and purging. Diuretics were considered a scurvy cure because they cleared the internal blockage that was causing the humoral imbalance. Although in retrospect Boerhaave's approach to the treatment of scurvy appears ill-founded and bizarre, he should not be judged solely on his opinions on this disease, which to him existed only in the realm of theory (since he lived in Leiden and never went to sea, and perhaps never personally observed a seriously scorbutic individual). Boerhaave made many contributions to medicine in his day, such as comparing the appearance of tissues and internal organs in a post-mortem autopsy with the cause of death. It was a baby step towards the empiricism that would transform the study of medicine in the coming century. Seventeenth- and early-eighteenth-century medicine was based not on scientific method or an experimental approach but on theoretical reconciliation. Fortunately for many patients, the humoral concept of medicine declined throughout the eighteenth century as physicians began studying the actual workings of internal organs and the circulatory system in greater detail. By the nineteenth century, medicine had returned to scientific ground, with an emphasis on observation and experiment rather than hypothesis and a desire for theoretical harmony.

In the 1600s and early 1700s, however, concurrent with a belief in the need to balance the four humours, there developed a belief that there was a universal cure to a universal disease. All diseases and their corresponding cures, went the argument, could and should be explained by a single theory. Diseases were not to be observed and treated independently but were supposed to fit within an overall theory that encompassed all human ailments—a universal law or set of principles for medicine similar to those then being developed for physics (such as Newton's laws of motion). A medical practitioner who observed that scurvy appeared when people had lived for prolonged periods of time on diets deficient in fresh fruits and vegetables, and who proposed that the cure would, therefore, be to eat more of these substances, would have had little respect within the medical community. How, after all, did this observation fit within the holistic network of the distempers that afflicted humanity? As it happens, an eighteenth-century Dutch physician, Johan Friedrich Bachstrom, did propose that scurvy was exclusively a deficiency disease, and he was dismissed for this precise reason.

Bachstrom was a Polish Lutheran pastor who later lived in Holland and England. At the urging of the Jesuits, he was imprisoned and died in Lithuania in 1742, at the age of fifty-six. He was the one light of the era who, more than any other writer for centuries before or decades after, truly understood scurvy as a deficiency disease. Bachstrom wrote of scurvy that "this evil is solely owing to a total abstinence from fresh vegetable food and greens, which is alone the true primary cause of the disease." He condemned the use of mer-

cury, alum, nitre, oil of vitriol, and other "mineral and fossil remedies," and then related a story, perhaps as a fable, of a sailor who
"was so over run and disabled with the scurvy" that his shipmates,
presuming his death, marooned him on the barren shores of Green-
land. The "poor wretch" crawled about the stony earth, "continually grazing like a beast of the field," until in a short time he was
miraculously cured and eventually returned home. The moral of the
story was that the eating of fresh vegetables promoted good health
and cured scurvy. Bachstrom divided plants into three broad and
crude categories, ranking their strength as antiscorbutics (a term he
coined to describe plants that would counter the effects of scurvy).
Bitter plants such as scurvy grass and cress he classified as the
strongest and most effective antiscorbutics; these were followed by
"sub-acid and acid" roots and berries, and then by plants and fruits
"of an insipid or rather sweetish taste." Although his rudimentary
classification system was in need of much improvement, he was
dead on when he proclaimed that "the most common herbs and
fresh fruits excel the most pompous pharmaceutical preparations."

Physicians, chemists, and theorists had by the early eighteenth
century succeeded in making scurvy so complicated and obtuse
that it would have been nearly impossible to get a useful or consistent
diagnosis from a physician. The world of medicine was extraordi-
narily confused, with a great variety of physicians each offering his
own personal variation on the humoral theory. To make universal
sense of it is nearly impossible; indeed, the theories of many physicians were contradictory. With the layers of speculation building
upon each other like the skins of an onion, and physicians tweaking
their predecessors' theories to accommodate glaring inconsistencies, scurvy and its causes and cures became ever more fanciful and
bewilderingly disconnected from reality. Gideon Harvey, the physician to Charles II, for example, pronounced in 1675 that there was
"a mouth scurvy, leg scurvy, joint scurvy, an asthmatic scurvy, a
rheumatic scurvy, a diarrhaeous scurvy, and emetic or vomiting

scurvy, a flatulent hypochondriac scurvy, a cutaneous scurvy, an ulcerous scurvy, a painful scurvy." In the quest for a universal theory of disease, much common sense was thrown aside and replaced with learned posturing. People, then as now, are inclined to dismiss trifling inconsistencies in their pet theories when they faithfully believe them to be correct—and perhaps more dangerous and malignant, when they believe a reputation is at stake or money is to be made. Folk wisdom has it that what we wish to be true, we readily believe. Whether this is universally applicable is debatable, but it must have played a role in the centuries-long saga to define and cure scurvy.

The now blindered theorizing of seventeenth- and eighteenth-century physicians resulted in some peculiar recommendations to the British Royal Navy (and probably the national navies of France, Holland, and Spain) from the medical establishment. Because of the social and educational distinctions between surgeons and physicians, the Admiralty always sought the advice of the College of Physicians in London or their own physician to the fleet over the opinions of the shipboard naval surgeons. These physicians were invariably educated at Edinburgh and indoctrinated in the theoretical foundations of medicine as propounded by Boerhaave. When the Admiralty asked them for advice on antiscorbutics, the results were predictable. In 1740, for example, the College of Physicians wrote to suggest that vinegar taken internally was "greatly conducive to the health of seamen, particularly in preventing scurvy." Presumably they meant an alkaline (or cold) scurvy that would be balanced by the acidity of the vinegar, which was considered to be warm and wet. Vinegar was still standard issue on navy ships decades after it had been proven to have no effect on scorbutic patients. On another occasion, the college informed the Admiralty, on identical theoretical grounds, that its members were "of the opinion that Elixir of Vitriol is an efficacious medicine and very proper to be a part of the invoice of the Surgeon's sea chest; they believe it often very useful in scorbutic cases." Similarly, it was possible for Anson's squadron, and all Royal Navy ships in 1753, to be supplied with the dangerous and violent Ward's Drop and Pill as an antiscorbutic because it was a purgative, and based on Boerhaave's theories it would clear the bowel blockage that was the underlying cause of the humoral imbalance that resulted in scurvy.

So instead of getting practical advice based on observation of actual conditions at sea, the Admiralty received theoretical pronouncements from non-naval academics who probably had never seen a case of severe scurvy and had no appreciation of a sailor's diet. They simply matched the stated symptoms with established and inflexible cures from a medical model that had been inherited from the Greeks and Romans thousands of years before. The formalization of medical thinking, education, and training stultified progress with useless theories and, when coupled with the centralization of victualling in national navies, made the prevention of scurvy nearly impossible. Just when expanding ship size, increasing time at sea, and the growing political importance of voyages made understanding and curing scurvy more important than ever, medical dogma got in the way.

By the eighteenth century, the theorists had succeeded in obfuscating with a bewildering fog of shifting hypotheses a problem that should have been, and indeed was at one time, solved by basic observation and common sense. Physicians would have been better off throwing out everything they had learned and starting over with basic, observable truths. It would take a remarkably bright and original thinker to even begin to deconstruct the intricate latticework of preposterous ideas to uncover the small kernel of truth that lay underneath it all. In 1753, a book was published that would begin this process. In it, an unassuming Scottish naval surgeon turned physician commented on the medical reasoning of the past century. "Theories were invented," he wrote, "galenical, chymical, and mechanical, according to the whim of each author, and the philosophy then in fashion. . . . The learned ignorance of the age lay concealed under a veil of unmeaning, unintelligible jargon. But, in order to make way for the restoration of solid learning, it was found necessary to expunge all such terms as were contrived to give an air of wisdom to the imperfections of knowledge."

Scurvy could not be cured or prevented so long as it was not understood. Fortunately for seafarers, by the middle of the 1700s the spirit of the age began to slowly shift away from placing trust in inherited truths and towards empirical experimentation and verifiable conclusions. One man in particular worked to rediscover the preventative for the disease that so ravaged the ranks of the Royal Navy.

5

AN OUNCE
OF PREVENTION:
JAMES LIND AND THE
SALISBURY EXPERIMENT

SOCIAL HIERARCHY aboard Royal Navy ships was rigid and strict. A ship's roster listed all hands, their positions and duties, and their pay. At the top, a virtual dictator with control literally over life and death, was the captain. He lived alone in a commodious private cabin at the stern of the ship. A red-coated marine stood guard at the entry to this illustrious compartment, where the captain hosted officers for formal dinners and conducted the vital business of running the ship. Next in line were the ship's lieutenants, usually aspiring younger men but occasionally an older man who, though trained and experienced enough to be a commander, lacked the social standing or funds to purchase his advancement. They ate their meals and spent most of their leisure time in the wardroom, which was situated in the stern, directly under the quarterdeck. Marine officers were also present on warships, and although they had no role in sailing the ship they dined with the other officers in the wardroom. One notch below the marine officers were the young gentlemen, or midshipmen, usually boys or young men who had not yet passed their exams for lieutenant.

The list of non-commissioned warrant officers was extensive. These included the purser (responsible for provisioning both the crew's food and the ship's supplies, such as spare timbers for masts, rope for rigging, tar, coal, and timber planks), the gunner, the carpenter, the cook (usually a disabled pensioner who had no cooking skills whatsoever), and the master (who was responsible for navigation and directing the course of the ship, but never for making important decisions). Ships also were manned with what could be termed civilian officers, such as schoolmasters, chaplains, and surgeons; they also dined with the officers in the wardroom, but they did not have the authority to command. Marines were also part of the ship's hierarchy, although their role was primarily to enforce the captain's authority and to act as troops during combat. Lower still, only one notch above the common sailors, was the surgeon's mate. The surgeon's mate dwelt within the bowels of the ship, in a six-foot-square canvas enclosure in the cockpit on the orlop deck, directly above the hold in the front of the vessel, where the rocking was greatest, the air foulest, and the natural light faintest. It was barely large enough to contain a sea chest and a medical chest, and the canvas walls pinned to the overhead beams provided scant privacy from the general crew. The surgeon's mate had no uniform, and though he was listed on the ship's roster alongside warrant officers such as the gunner or the carpenter, he received less pay. Neither surgeons nor surgeon's mates were highly regarded in the naval hierarchy, since the health of the crews was of little consideration and the benefits not entirely understood or appreciated.

It was as a surgeon's mate that James Lind entered the Royal Navy in 1739. Although it was not a prestigious or well-compensated position, it was one of the best ways for a young medical professional without influential family connections to gain experience. Lind was born the second child and first son of a well-to-do family of middle-class merchants in Edinburgh on October 4, 1716. He was well educated from a young age and perhaps took his interest in medicine from an uncle who was a physician. When he was fifteen years old he was apprenticed to a well-known Edinburgh physician and surgeon named George Langlands. By then he had acquired a solid foundation in Latin and Greek, the universal languages of learned professionals, particularly in medicine, and at least a reading knowledge of French and German. For eight years he learned the practical trade of a surgeon from Langlands, dressing and cleaning wounds, setting bones, mixing drugs, and letting blood. He studied the theoretical side of medicine under the handful of young physicians who had recently begun teaching at the University of Edinburgh.

These young and energetic physicians, who were appointed by the town council as "Professors in the University," had all studied in Leiden, Holland, under the famous Dr. Hermann Boerhaave. They established the medical tradition at the University of Edinburgh and provided Lind with the theoretical and academic grounding that gave structure to his future studies. Langlands, coincidentally, was also a student of Boerhaave's, as were most of the respected Edinburgh physicians at that time. Whether he agreed with them or not, Lind spent years learning Boerhaave's theories on the humoral concept of disease, and they became the lens through which he viewed medical problems, including scurvy.

Although Lind began as a lowly surgeon's apprentice, from an early age it was clear he had much grander ambitions. He studied languages and expressed an interest in medical theories, rather than concentrating purely on surgical work. In the eighteenth century there was a distinct separation between physicians, who concerned themselves with internal bodily functions and the theory of disease, and surgeons, who were concerned with fractures, cuts, and other physical injuries that could be helped by manipulation. Physicians were more educated and held a much higher social status than surgeons. They earned more money and generally belonged to more respectable or richer families.

Lind's surgical apprenticeship was more or less complete in 1739—the year Spain and England declared war and Anson began organizing his voyage. Rather than setting up a private practice in Edinburgh, difficult for a young, relatively inexperienced man, he applied to join the Royal Navy as a surgeon's mate. A majority of surgeons in the Royal Navy at this time hailed from Scotland. Lind had no degree from his years of training, but this was not uncommon. He easily passed his examination at Surgeons' Hall and was declared morally, physically, and professionally competent for the navy. For seven years he laboured as a lowly surgeon's mate, learning the trade of a naval surgeon. "To the surgeon's mate fell the most arduous duties and menial tasks," wrote an early biographer of Lind's named Edward Hudson. "He would boil the gruel, barley water, and fomentations, wash the towels and dressings, prepare and change dressings, mix and spread plasters, fill and carry the patients' water buckets, sweep out the sick bay, and often be required to empty the buckets used as commodes. He was at the beck and call of the ship's surgeon twenty-four hours a day." It was also his duty to muster the sick each morning. A ship's boy sauntered about the decks, ringing the sick bell and mustering the men for sick call, which was held in fine weather before the mast just below the quarterdeck. Anyone who was sick or injured presented himself to the surgeon and captain, justified and explained his injuries, and asked to be excused from his regular duties. The captain, in his impressive ceremonial uniform, with cocked hat athwart and sabre casually dangling (a uniform that cost as much as or more than the seaman's annual salary), attended the muster to discourage sailors from faking illness and shirking duty (which was believed to be widespread in the navy but probably wasn't, since sick mariners had their meagre pay docked and were sometimes charged for medications).

In the evening the surgeon's mate made a round of the ship, inspecting the invalids in their quarters if they were officers or warrant officers and in the sick bay if they were common sailors. The sick bay was a damp, crowded, musty cell below the waterline where the fetid airs lingered and dim, smouldering lanterns provided the only light. The patients hung in hammocks suspended row upon row several deep with little over a foot of space between them. In turbulent weather they might knock against each other. Sanitation was non-existent, and the patients, no matter their sickness or wounds, breathed the stale air and exhalations of their comrades, likely infecting each other and generally impeding any chance of quick recovery. In 1748 Tobias Smollett, who had entered the navy the same year as Lind, wrote *Roderick Random*, his classic tale of the life of a surgeon's mate. It was a lurid and exaggerated account of the dreadful and morbid conditions aboard ships and the state of medicine. His description of the sick bay is a revealing, if overdone, account of what Lind himself would have been exposed to. "Here I saw fifty miserable distempered wretches, suspended in rows," he wrote, "so huddled one upon another, that not more than fourteen inches space was allotted for each with his bed and bedding; and deprived of the light of day, as well as fresh air; each patient breathing nothing but a noisome atmosphere of the morbid steams exhaling from their own excrements and diseased bodies, devoured with vermin hatched in the filth that surrounded them, and destitute of every convenience necessary for people in that helpless condition."

It must have been a startling and eye-opening initiation into the world for a twenty-three-year-old man from Edinburgh who had never been away from land before. Since Lind never wrote a memoir, we have no record of what he thought of this rude introduction to the harsh reality of life at sea—the foul food, stagnant water, harsh discipline, and, most important from a medical point of view, innumerable ailments from battle, fevers, and accidents. He dealt with

Sick Bay
H.M. Hero. Nov. 14 1860.

In the Age of Sail, the sick bay in a ship of the line was a damp, crowded, musty cell below the waterline in fetid air with dim smoldering lanterns providing the only light. Sanitation was non-existent, and the patients breathed the stale air and exhalations of their comrades, likely infecting each other and impeding any chance of quick recovery.

the standard problems that are likely to arise in a group of several hundred close-quartered men of below-average health, pulling teeth, setting bones, issuing painkillers, treating venereal disease or the dreaded yellow fever, and calming those suffering from battle-induced dementia. He would have been able to saw off a mangled limb with good speed, quickly stitch up a gaping wound, realign a crushed leg bone, and, most important, know when a patient was beyond the help of his rudimentary medical abilities and call in the chaplain.

Naval records show that Lind participated in at least one battle, the attack on the Spanish island of Minorca in 1739, and he likely experienced many other instances where storms, minor skirmishes, serious shipboard accidents, or infectious diseases laid low significant portions of the crew. During battle he would have joined the surgeon in the cockpit or sick bay, awaiting the wounded. As a surgeon's mate he would have readied the battle dressing station, ensuring it was well stocked and supplied, and assisted the surgeon in any capacity required. The dressing station contained "water, lint, dressings, sponges, tourniquets, buckets of sand to absorb blood, tables for operating, and for instruments, a chest of drugs, and blankets on which to lay the wounded." After several years of merely assisting, he might have actually completed his own surgeries. Following a battle, the cockpit was like a slaughterhouse. Screeching men—some with mangled or severed limbs, others with great oak splinters protruding from them, and still others with hideous burns—were brought down into the gloom, many never to return to the world above. Blood spattered over everything as the surgeons gouged into flesh to remove splinters and sawed and cut through bone and muscle. Wounds were cauterized with boiling tar.

The survival rate for serious injuries was very low, sterilization and anaesthetics other than rum non-existent, and surgical techniques in their infancy. It must have taken a philosophical and

practical mind to have thrived under such conditions. But thrive
Lind must have, for not only was he promoted to ship's surgeon but
he eventually rose to become a prominent Edinburgh physician
and then head of England's largest and newest hospital. During his
long years in the Royal Navy, on voyages to the West Indies, the
Mediterranean, and western Africa, Lind learned the surgeon's job
well and spent considerable time observing shipboard conditions,
undoubtedly laying the foundation for all his later studies and writings on naval hygiene and sea diseases. He synthesized a great deal
of information during his tenure at sea. Many of his later essays and
books are cogent and useful; they show a clear mind and a desire
to understand the root of problems instead of being intoxicated by
the heady vapours of theory so prevalent at that time. In his lowly
capacity as surgeon's mate, it is unlikely he ever made his opinions
known—except perhaps in his own journal, which he was under a
professional obligation to keep and which would have been carefully scrutinized by the medical examining board before he was
promoted. Lind was a physician at heart, intrigued much more by
the peculiar puzzle of understanding the causes of and cures for disease than by the mere treatment of physical wounds.

In late 1746, Lind turned in his medical and surgical journals
and passed his examinations for surgeon. He was promoted aboard
HMS *Salisbury*, for a round of duty in the English Channel and the
Mediterranean. The *Salisbury* was a fourth-rate ship—that is to say,
it was the smallest of ships considered ships of the line, or battleships, and just larger than the fifth or sixth rates, which were considered frigates. While the largest ships boasted more than one
hundred great guns, with a displacement of 2,000 to 2,600 tons
and capable of holding 850 to 1,000 sailors, the fourth-rate *Salisbury* had 50 to 60 great guns, was about 1,100 tons, and held about
350 mariners. It might have been only 150 feet long, making for very
cramped living conditions and little privacy. Although it was not
the largest ship Lind had served aboard, it was still a huge vessel,

and because of its size it afforded an array of sick sailors, including a large contingent of scorbutic patients who began to show symptoms several months into the tour of duty.

As ship's surgeon, Lind, now thirty-one years old and competent by naval standards, dreamt up a remarkable scheme that reveals a great deal about his analytical and practical mind. Scurvy was no stranger to Lind after eight years in the navy, and as surgeon he would have been directly responsible for ministering to mariners down with the affliction. Scurvy probably reared up in every ship he served on, though there is no record of whether he himself suffered from it. Lind would have been familiar with all the common "cures," and aware also that they seldom had any beneficial effect. Accordingly, showing an astonishing propensity for originality, for thinking outside the strict lines of contemporary thought, he planned an experiment to test and evaluate the effectiveness of the most common antiscorbutics. He was fortunate that his captain, the Honourable George Edgecombe, was a fellow of the Royal Society whose scientific interests meshed with his own. Lind could not have conducted his experiment without the complicity, or at least the blessing, of his captain. Many naval captains would not have been so open to new ideas, and most never would have permitted Lind the time and resources to conduct his experiment.

During April and May of 1747, the HMS *Salisbury* cruised the English Channel with the other ships of the Channel fleet. Though the ship was never far from land, scurvy began its insidious appearance. More than four hundred of the fleet's four thousand mariners were showing symptoms, and most of the regular crew of the *Salisbury* were affected to some extent, with nearly eighty seriously weakened. On May 20, Lind, with the agreement of his enlightened captain, though not necessarily with the consent of the scorbutic sailors, took aside twelve men with advanced symptoms of scurvy "as similar as I could have them." They "all in general had putrid gums, the spots and lassitude, with weakness of their knees."

Lind hung their hammocks in a separate compartment in the fore-hold—as dank, dark, and cloying as can be imagined—and provided "one diet common to all." Breakfast consisted of gruel sweetened with sugar. Lunch (or dinner) was either "fresh mutton broth" or occasionally "puddings, boiled biscuit with sugar." And for supper he had the cook prepare barley and raisins, rice and currants, sago and wine. Lind also controlled the quantities of food eaten. During the fourteen-day period, he separated the scorbutic sailors into six pairs and supplemented the diet of each pair with various antiscorbutic medicines and foods.

The first pair were ordered a quart of "cyder" (slightly alcoholic) per day. The second pair were administered twenty-five "guts" (drops) of elixir of vitriol three times daily on an empty stomach and also "using a gargle strongly acidulated with it for their mouths." A third pair took two spoonfuls of vinegar three times daily, also on an empty stomach, also gargling with it and having their food liberally doused with it. The fourth pair, who were the two most severely suffering patients, "with the tendons in the ham rigid," were given the seemingly oddest treatment: sea water, of which they drank "half a pint every day, and sometimes more or less as it operated, by way of a general physic." The fifth set of sailors each were fed two oranges and one lemon daily for six days, when the ship's meagre supply ran out. The sixth pair were ordered an "electuary" (medicinal paste), "the bigness of a nutmeg," thrice daily. The paste consisted of garlic, mustard seed, dried radish root, balsam of Peru, and gum myrrh. It was washed down with barley water "well acidulated with tamarinds." And on several occasions they were fed cream of tartar, a mild laxative, "by which they were gently purged three or four times during the course." Lind also kept several scorbutic sailors aside in a different room and gave them nothing beyond the standard naval diet other than the occasional "lenitive electuary" (painkiller) and cream of tartar.

This experiment was one of the first controlled trials in medical history, or in any branch of clinical science. The results were surprising. The lucky pair who were fed the oranges and lemons (which, according to Lind, they "ate greedily") were nearly completely recovered by the time the fruit supply dwindled after only a week. One of the men responded to the treatment so remarkably that although the "spots were not indeed at that time quite off his body, nor his gums sound," he returned to duty after a gargle of elixir (oil) of vitriol. He was followed soon thereafter by his companion, and both were then "appointed nurse to the rest of the sick" for the remainder of the trial.

Those who had drunk the cider also responded favourably, but at the end of two weeks they were still too weak to return to duty. Still, they showed slight improvement, such that "the putrefaction of their gums, but especially their lassitude and weakness, were somewhat abated." On an earlier voyage Lind had observed that cider did not fend off the advances of scurvy but seemed to slow its progress. A great number of sailors lingered long in sickness but did not perish as quickly as those who were not drinking cider, or who were drinking beer or rum punch instead. Modern researchers have shown that cider, particularly if not overly purified, pasteurized, or stored for too long, does contain small quantities of ascorbic acid, and therefore could have been a mild preventative. The unfortunate men who gargled and drank the elixir of vitriol found their mouths "much cleaner and in better condition than the rest," but Lind "perceived otherwise no good effects from its internal use upon the other symptoms." He also observed no positive effects from the vinegar, the sea water, or the electuary-and-tamarind concoction. His conclusion was that "the most sudden and visible good effects were perceived from the use of the oranges and lemons. . . . Oranges and lemons were the most effectual remedies for this distemper at sea."

Most unusual was Lind's decision to give sea water to the two worst cases in his trial. He suspected, or hoped, that the easily obtainable sea water would prove to be beneficial—certainly this would have been excellent news to the Admiralty, as it was both cheap and of infinite supply. Lind later wrote of hearing tales of "numberless instances of giving salt water in very bad scurvies . . . with great benefit." Sea water was still pronounced a viable and effective scurvy cure years later—in published accounts by professional physicians. In Lind's official trial, however, he found that it had no effect whatsoever—not surprising from a modern viewpoint, but perhaps disappointing to Lind. Elixir of vitriol was the most commonly issued antiscorbutic medicine used by the Royal Navy at the time, so for Lind also to have proven it entirely ineffective was a small advancement in itself, although it took six years of work before he published any of his findings, and even then, in spite of his seemingly clear proof, not everyone agreed with his conclusions.

In 1748, hostilities between England and Spain abated and Lind retired from the Royal Navy, on half pay for a number of years. He returned to Edinburgh, where he set out to complete his medical degree, producing a hastily researched and written thesis on venereal lesions titled *De morbis venereis localibus*, which proved adequate to satisfy the requirements. That same year he became "a Graduate Doctor of Medicine in the University of Edinburgh." With a licence from the Royal College of Physicians to practise "within the City of Edinburgh & Liberty ye of without any tryal or Examination," he began to offer his services to the city and surrounding region on May 3, 1748. In his quiet, unpretentious manner, he thrived by virtue of good work and a dedication to his profession.

In 1750, Lind was elected a fellow of the Royal College of Physicians of Edinburgh. His private practice was thriving. He was a private man with little interest in attracting public attention, and very little is known of his personal life, other than that he was extremely dedicated and hard-working, often continuing his scurvy research in the evenings after he left his office. Judging by the competence he later showed as a hospital administrator, and the thoroughness of his essays and books, we can conclude that he was a conscientious and responsible physician, willing to admit when an illness eluded his understanding—not necessarily the norm for the time. It was during his tenure in Edinburgh that he married a woman named Isobel Dickie. Little is known about her other than that she died two years after Lind, on March 6, 1796, at the age seventy-six—so she was in her late twenties or early thirties when they wed and would have likely come from a well-established middle-class family. The couple had one son, named John, who also became a surgeon and a physician.

After several years of working towards professional respectability and financial stability, Lind began to write an essay about his *Salisbury* trial and his observations on scurvy. When the voluminous information began to overwhelm him, he decided to turn his essay into a comprehensive book. He spent years collecting every known description of scurvy, from ancient times to the most recent, writing hundreds of letters to foreign colleagues, acquiring documents from around Europe and either translating them himself or having copies translated for him. The work contained a great *bibliotheca scorbutica*, a collection and review of every medical opinion and account of the disease that Lind could unearth. This in itself was no small task for a working doctor to do in his spare time, without reliable mail service and modern telecommunications tools. "What was intended," he wrote, "as a short paper to be published in the memoirs of our medical naval society . . . swelled to a volume."

It was not until 1753 that Lind's *Treatise on the Scurvy, Containing an Inquiry into the Nature, Causes, and Cure, of That Disease Together with a Critical and Chronological View of What Has Been Published on the Subject* appeared in Edinburgh. Other editions in other countries and languages soon followed. Six years had passed since he had conducted his controlled trial aboard the *Salisbury*, but the incidence of scurvy in the Royal Navy had not changed in the slightest during the intervening years. Lind dedicated his work to "The Rt. Hon. George, Lord Anson," who was at that time, a decade after his historic cruise in pursuit of the Manila galleon in the Pacific, the influential First Lord of the Admiralty. The published account of Anson's voyage was released in 1748, the year Lind left the Royal Navy, and there is little doubt that Lind read the account, and that it stimulated his further inquiry into scurvy while he was in Edinburgh. Lind wrote in the preface to the first edition of his treatise that "after the publication of the Right Honourable Lord Anson's voyage, by the Reverend Mr. Walter, the lively and elegant picture there exhibited of the distress occasioned by this disease, which afflicted the crews of that noble, brave, and experienced Commander . . . excited the curiosity of many to inquire into the nature of a malady accompanied with such extraordinary appearances." He was aware of the terrible toll scurvy took on Anson's crew, and it was one of the main reasons he began anew his studies into the dreaded disease.

The treatise was a four-hundred-page tome that, in addition to presenting a comprehensive list and analysis of current and historical theories and cures for scurvy, outlined Lind's strong personal opinions on the benefits of a cure not only for individual sailors but for the Royal Navy and England in general. In case others had not yet grasped the significance, Lind spent considerable time making his case before launching into his assessment of the disease's causes, prevention, and cure. Lind made his plea: "Common humanity ever pleads for the Afflicted. . . . But, surely, there are no lives more valuable to the State, or who have a better claim to its care, than those of the British sailors to whom the Nation, in great measure owes its Riches, Protection, and Liberties."

Lind also wrote in his preface that "the scurvy alone, during the last war, proved a more destructive enemy, and cut off more valuable

TRAITÉ
DU
SCORBUT,
DIVISÉ EN TROIS PARTIES,
CONTENANT

Des recherches fur la nature , les caufes
& la curation de cette Maladie.

*Avec un Tableau chronologique & critique de
tout ce qui a paru fur ce fujet.*

Traduit de l'Anglois de M. LIND, D. M. Membre
du Collége Royal de Médecine d'Edimbourg.

*Auquel on a joint la Traduction du Traité du Scorbut
de* BOERHAAVE, *commenté par M.* VAN SWIETEN.

TOME PREMIER.

A PARIS,

Chez GANEAU , Libraire , rue Saint Severin ;
aux Armes de Dombes.

M. DCC. LVI.

Avec Approbation & Privilége du Roi.

The title page of an early French edition of Lind's *Treatise on the Scurvy*,
showing the influence of Hermann Boerhaave in mid-18th century medical circles.

lives, than the united efforts of the French and Spanish arms." The statistics on the incidence of scurvy in the Royal Navy during the Seven Years' War a decade later, when more accurate records were kept, corroborate Lind's claim. In hindsight, it seems preposterous that a sickness that was the acknowledged cause of such devastating loss of life and such a drain on naval power could be allowed to go so long without government intervention, but in the mid-eighteenth century the benefits of a healthy crew were not entirely appreciated by those in command, and prevention was considered a foolish waste of resources and time. Lind was clearly interested in preventative, rather than curative, medicine—if the distemper could be prevented, he reasoned, it need not be cured. But in this he was far ahead of his time. Ignorance of medical matters was rife in the officers' ranks, as medical approaches and concerns were not part of their training.

Lind explained in his treatise that even when scurvy didn't directly claim the lives of crew members, it weakened them, hindering their ability to do their duty with vigour and withstand other diseases. Scurvy, he wrote, "has not only occasionally committed surprising ravages in ships and fleets, but almost always affects the constitution of sailors; and where it does not rise to any visible calamity, yet it often makes a powerful addition to the malignity of other diseases." It was a perceptive and accurate observation based on his years at sea. After outlining the benefits of finding a cure, Lind described in detail the particulars of his clinical trial aboard the *Salisbury* (including his conclusion that oranges and lemons were the best cures), and then listed his other suggestions for staving off the affliction and offered his theory of the disease.

Lind's detailed analysis of the explanations for scurvy found in ancient and more recent works was unusually cogent, and reading it would have given any physician a solid understanding of what was then known of the disease. It is a literature review of the period up to 1753. "Before this subject could be set in a clear and proper light," he claimed, perhaps as a justification for the years he spent collecting and reviewing every description of scurvy he could find, "it was necessary to remove a great deal of rubbish." Much of what had been proposed by medical thinkers up to that point, and regrettably beyond, was indeed rubbish, and it could not possibly have been based on anything other than personal opinion or fashion.

Lind apologized to the many "eminent and learned authors" whose work he criticized, claiming that it was done not with "a malignant view of deprecating their labours, but from regard to truth and to the good of mankind." For one prominent seventeenth-century Dutch writer, Severinus Euglenus, who attributed a great many ailments to the "scorbutic taint," Lind reserved particular ire, claiming that "his vanity and presumption are indeed intolerable." The disease was caused, according to Euglenus, by "divine permission, as chastisement for the sins of the world." Certain men, Lind caustically observed, continued to follow Euglenus's lead, and "they even exceed him in absurdities."

Lind's criticism of the many preposterous theories was a refreshing departure from the stultifying uniformity of medical thought at the time, and his insistence on having evidence and proof before accepting the validity of a theory ought to have been common practice. From a modern perspective, one wonders how it couldn't have been. His clinical trial, although crude and rudimentary by modern standards, was a true advancement. There are examples of a handful of clinical trials dating from as early as the eleventh century, but somehow the concept never took hold. So it is all the more saddening and curious that, after providing a balanced and thorough critique of the medical theories on scurvy, a concise diagnosis of its symptoms and progression, and accurate and effective suggestions for cures, Lind then becomes derailed with a verbose and gaseous theoretical pronouncement on scurvy's cause.

His complicated and peculiar theory is difficult to correlate even with his own observations. Perhaps Lind's greatest failing was that he didn't turn his own critical analysis, so effectively deployed to demolish the erroneous presumptions of other physicians, on himself. Lind's theory of the cause of scurvy is as preposterous and harebrained as any of the theories he so eloquently criticized. It seems to have been pulled from the air. Although it is difficult to coherently summarize, his convoluted and ornate argument is basically that scurvy is caused by blockage of the body's natural perspiration, which leads to an imbalance in the body's alkalinity. This unfortunate imbalance, he claimed, is caused by the dampness at sea and aboard ships. Although Lind had proven by trial and error that fresh greens and citrus fruits were the most effective antiscorbutics, his analysis of the root causes of scurvy was, unfortunately, an elaborate and foolish guess. It is easy to see Boerhaave's influence on his theory of disease, though Lind mercifully put no stock in the malignant properties of foul vapours and he never referred to the spleen.

"An animal body," Lind begins, "is composed of solid and fluid parts; and these consist of such various and heterogeneous principles, as render it, of all substances, the most liable to corruption and putrefaction. . . . For by the uninterrupted circulation of its fluids, their violent attrition, and mutual actions on each other, and their containing vessels, the whole mass of humours is apt to degenerate from its sweet, mild, and healthful condition, into various degrees of acrimony and corruption. . . . The most considerable of all the evacuations, is that by insensible perspiration; which Sanctorius found in Italy to be equal to five eighths of the meat and drink taken into the body. . . . And it is certain these excrementitious humours naturally destined for this evacuation, when retained long in the body, are capable of acquiring the most poisonous and noxious qualities . . . becoming extremely acrid and corrosive: and do then give rise to various diseases."

If another physician had produced such a theory, Lind would likely have dissected it and dismissed it as "a great deal of rubbish." But he probably felt that he needed an important-sounding theory in order to be taken seriously in the medical community, which at this time conducted discourse in complicated, imprecise language. Perhaps Lind even believed this argument—though it runs counter to his rigorous observations and analysis of the work of others. Under his theory, all acids would have been scurvy cures, yet his own trial showed conclusively that vitriol and vinegar had no effect whatsoever on scorbutic patients. Oddly, Lind even acknowledged the flaws in his own reasoning. "For some might naturally conclude," he admits, "that oranges and lemons are but so many acids, for which, vinegar, vitriol, etc. would prove excellent substitutes. But, upon bringing this to the test of experience, we find the contrary. Few ships have ever been in want of vinegar, and, for many years were supplied with vitriol. Yet the Channel fleet often had a thousand men miserably over-run with this disease. . . . Although acids agree in certain properties, yet they differ widely in others, and especially in their effects upon the human body." Lind was confused, and as he attempted to patch up each new unravelling thread in the fabric of his theory, it became more and more difficult to reconcile with common sense. After acknowledging that, theoretical similarities aside, certain acids had a special "other property," he failed to show what this other property was.

Lind's greatest failure was his attempt to conform to the prevailing intellectual model for the theory of disease. To be respected by his medical peers, he had to explain scurvy and show how it fit within the greater framework of disease in general—to devise a theory that would apply not only in specific cases but could be the foundation for an understanding of all ailments of the human body. With such a lofty objective for medicine at the time, it is no wonder Lind failed to squeeze every symptom and observation into a grand synthesis of all sickness. He fell prey to the same tendency to theorize that he dismissed in others, and yet he seems to have been aware of his own failings. "Of theory in physic," he admits, "the same may perhaps be said, as has been observed by some of zeal in religion, that it is indeed absolutely necessary yet, by carrying it too far, it may be doubted whether it has done more good or hurt in the world." While Lind came upon the cure for the disease, he was simply incapable, because of a lack of resources, knowledge, and the insight of other scientists, of deriving the cause. Taking his study further was beyond his capacity at that time.

For various reasons, not the least of which might have been Lind's own convoluted theories of the causes of scurvy and his inability to explain why orange and lemon juice should cure the sickness, his recommendation for citrus juice as a preventative and his assertion that oil of vitriol had no antiscorbutic properties were not heeded. His practical cure was lost in the cloud of theories, including his own. Within a few years of the publication of Lind's treatise, several other physicians produced essays that directly contradicted his suggestions, even for a cure. The lack of enthusiasm for Lind's ideas within the medical community, which was caused by his own impolitic, though honest, criticisms of his peers, might also have delayed the acceptance of his conclusions. Lind didn't shy from criticizing his contemporaries. Two men in particular did not appreciate his trampling on their turf.

In the same year that Lind's treatise was published, a well-known and influential physician named Anthony Addington, a man who walked in high circles, as personal physician to William Pitt, the prime minister, and was well acquainted with several lords of the Admiralty from his Oxford days, published *An Essay on the Sea Scurvy: Wherein Is Proposed an Easy Method of Curing That Distemper at Sea, and of Preserving Water Sweet for Any Cruize or Voyage.* He dedicated his book to all seven lords of the Admiralty by name. It was an unusual tome from a man whose specialty was in mental disorders, and who had never gone to sea. His description and

analysis of scurvy was based on the very accounts Lind had criticized. Compared with Lind's clear analysis of the symptoms and
progression of the disease, Addington's seems unlikely to have been
published contemporaneously. "In the last stage," Addington
writes, "which is contagious, [scurvy] produces horrors of imagination; trembling, panting, convulsive, epileptic fits; weakness of
memory and reason, lethargies, palsies, apoplexies; purple, livid and
black spots; violent effusion of blood from every internal and ex-
ternal part of the body; putrid fevers, hectic, continued and inter-
mittent: exquisite rheumatic pains, pleurisies, the jaundice, obstinate
costiveness, colics, vomiting, diarrheas, dysenteries, mortifications."
One wonders, in Addington's world, what symptoms were not the
result of scurvy. Nevertheless, the influential doctor pronounced
with authority that the best scurvy cures were sea water—both for
drinking and for purging—and bloodletting, to reduce the hemorrhaging. To preserve sea water and prevent it from going putrid, and
thereby contributing to scurvy, he proposed adding hydrochloric
acid to a small quantity and then blending it with the ship's drinking water.

Lind's treatise was published only a few months after Addington's
essay, and Lind was not overly kind in his assessment of Addington's analysis, dismissing it as valueless and ill-founded, which it
was. A. P. Meiklejohn wrote in 1951, in the *Journal of the History of
Medicine*, that "though there is no record of his [Addington's] opinion of Lind, it was unlikely to have been favourable and somewhere,
at some time, this might well have told against Lind."

Lind also had a sour relationship with Charles Bisset, a peer
and acquaintance from his days as a student in Edinburgh. Unlike
Addington, Bisset had considerable experience at sea and in treating
naval disorders. In 1755 he released *A Treatise on the Scurvy, Designed
Chiefly for the Use of the British Navy*, a tract influenced by Lind's
treatise and designed to counter what he considered Lind's erroneous position. Bisset proposed that scurvy could take one of several

distinct manifestations, including "Malignant, Continued, Remit-
ting and Intermitting Fevers and Fluxes" and scorbutic ulcers. He
claimed as scorbutic many symptoms that clearly were not scurvy.
The core of Bisset's belief was that solar heat weakens the "vital
powers," and that they become "unequal to the density and tenacity
of the gross navy-victuals: the animal juices which they prepare
from this ailment are therefore crude, viscid, light and unequally
mixed: the bile, and other chylopoietic juices become too oily, and
much depraved: the ingested rancid oil of meat that is tainted retains
its nature, and contributed with reassumed and acrid animal oil, to
increase the unequal and preternatural mixture, and depravity of
the circulating juices."

It would be a painful task to try to clearly summarize the entirety
of Bisset's ponderous and pedantic argument, much of which appears
designed to impress the reader with his use of uncommon, learned
words. But on one point he is unmistakably clear: James Lind is
not to be credited with understanding scurvy. "Dr. Lind reckons
the want of fresh vegetables and greens a very powerful cause of the
scurvy," he writes condescendingly. "He might, with equal reason,
have added fresh animal food, wine, punch, spruce beer, or whatever else is capable of preventing this disease." Bisset, not surprisingly, had his own recommendation for the greatest antiscorbutic:
rum or other suitable hard liquor, diluted with water and laced with
sugar. Sugar "renders more aperient, detersive, and less heating,
and highly antiscorbutic: for sugar, notwithstanding the groundless
prejudice which many entertain against it, is aperient, detersive,
demulcent, antiseptic, and consequently an excellent medicine
against the scurvy." Bisset also believed that rice has "very powerful
antiscorbutic and restorative qualities." Lind never responded to
Bisset's treatise.

Bisset's antipathy to Lind might have arisen out of a difference in
political leanings. While Bisset served in the army on the Hanoverian side to repel Charles Edward Stuart's rebellion in Scotland in

1745, Lind was likely a closet Jacobite. Although Lind never took part in any battles of the Jacobite rebellion, or left any record of his sympathies, A. P. Meiklejohn observed that "when the time came to have his portrait painted it was done, not by one of the great portrait artists of the day, but by a dispossessed Scottish Jacobite, Sir George Chalmers." Bisset also had influential friends within the scientific and medical community, not the least of whom was the aristocratic Scottish physician Dr. (later Sir) John Pringle.

Pringle was at various times throughout his career the surgeon general of the English army, physician to King George III, and author of the groundbreaking book *Observations on the Diseases of the Army*, in which he emphasized sanitation and hygiene to improve the health of soldiers. Pringle also pioneered the concept that hospitals should be respected as sanctuaries by both sides during war. His clients included nobility and the influential lords of the realm. Even before he became president of the Royal Society in 1772, he was a man with clout, social stature, and influence. Pringle took a great interest in James Cook's voyages and in scurvy throughout the 1770s, and he had considerable influence on the Admiralty's choice of antiscorbutics during the era of the War of American Independence.

Men like Addington and Bisset were respected and influential, more so than Lind, and it is not surprising that in that day and age, when connections and social standing frequently counted for more than competence, their claims, pronounced without a shred of verifiable evidence, were given the same consideration as Lind's. But Lind's remarkable trial aboard the HMS *Salisbury* at least set a foot on the path to finally understanding scurvy—the evidence of his trial was published and available for others to read.

Before Lind's experiments, scurvy was not clearly defined as a disease. The term was used as a catchphrase to include all manner of nautical ailments. The seventeenth-century naval surgeon John Hall wrote in *The Power of Water Dock against Scurvy* that "if anyone is ill, and knows not his Disease, Let him suspect the scurvy." Nevertheless, for years after Lind's treatise was published, scurvy remained as much a problem as ever. But slowly the Admiralty began to take a greater interest in solving the scurvy problem. The growing body of information that painted scurvy, "this foul and fatal mischief," as the greatest of all obstacles to the navy's objectives was becoming too large to ignore, and the implications of not solving the problem were becoming increasingly significant.

Unfortunately, it was more than the preposterous foundations of medical reasoning that hampered the study of the disease. Lind had difficulty determining the exact cause of scurvy in part because mariners suffered from so many other diseases and dietary deficiencies that isolating the symptoms of one condition was a complex and bewildering task. But the officers and young gentlemen aboard ships suffered far less from scurvy than the general crew, and Lind speculated that this was at least partly because of their better overall health and diet.

While Lind recognized that the lack of fresh provisions was directly linked to scurvy, he also advocated warmth, proper rest, and proper ventilation in ships—all things that would no doubt have benefited the average sailor, reducing the body's rate of consumption of ascorbic acid. But they would have been insufficient to cure or prevent scurvy on prolonged voyages. Lind knew instinctively that conditions inherent to a life at sea during the Age of Sail, such as cold, damp, infection, alcohol, discontent, and stress, directly contributed to scurvy. "As the atmosphere at sea may always be supposed to be moister than that of the land," he wrote, "hence there is always a greater disposition to the scorbutic diathesis at sea than in a pure dry land air." Life at sea was harsh and cruel and lonely, and Lind was very perceptive when he observed that it strengthened the clutches of scurvy.

In 1757, Lind, continuing his work on naval hygiene and disease and revealing his sympathy for the plight of the average seaman and the atrocious conditions in the Royal Navy, wrote a second book, called *An Essay on the Most Effectual Means of Preserving the Health of Seamen in the Royal Navy*. In this essay, Lind defined what he believed to be the responsibility of a naval surgeon, and he outlined his suggestions for ameliorating the harsh and foul conditions for common sailors aboard ships. He further developed his view that preventing disease was far more advantageous than curing it, and that cleanliness and better conditions for mariners would not only reduce the incidence of scurvy but aid in limiting other diseases as well. "The Prophylactic or preventative branch of medical science does," Lind wrote, "in many instances, admit of as much, or even more certainty, than the curative part. . . . A medicine, which effectually prevents, deserves to be more esteemed than that which merely removes. . . . With regard to the Royal Navy, when men are preserved in health by proper management; Courage and Activity are the certain consequences."

Perhaps most significantly, Lind argued for the quarantine of newly impressed sailors and convicts released from prison to prevent the new recruits from bringing infectious fevers into the crowded ships. He also accurately pointed out that the practice of loading a ship with double the number of mariners needed to sail it was a major cause of high mortality rates from disease. Crowded ships and poor hygiene fed on one another. Without good hygiene and proper food, Lind wrote, the navy would continue to need the extra men because they would continue to die at alarming rates. He was the first medical writer to point this out. Lind's essay was a remarkably enlightened social document for the time, so it is unfortunate that most of his recommendations were ignored for many years.

Although Lind never returned to sea, he had an opportunity, perhaps unequalled by any other physician in Europe, to study scorbutic patients and other naval diseases. In 1758, he was appointed chief physician to the Royal Naval Hospital at Haslar, the largest and newest hospital in the country.

UNWINDING THE KNOT: ROB AND WORT AND THE TRIALS AT SEA

A PORTRAIT OF LIND in middle age shows him as an ascetic but amiable academic with a ruffled and coiffed wig, floppy cuffs, and a vest stretched over a slight paunch. Although he sits straight, his shoulders are stooped as if from many hours of reading or working by dim light. A high forehead and clear eyes are counterbalanced by a tight, knowing smile. He is a man of books, and in his hands he clutches a copy of an early edition of his own famous text, the groundbreaking but underappreciated *Treatise on the Scurvy*. Clearly pleased with his status as head of Haslar, England's most prestigious hospital, he is posed with the building in the background. He had been appointed head because of his interest in scurvy and the health of sailors. An appointment of such distinction and salary would not have been made based on merit alone—some form of patronage would have been needed, and historians have proposed that this must have come from Lord Anson himself. Anson had maintained an active interest in naval disease in general, and scurvy in particular, since becoming First Lord of the Admiralty in 1751.

Haslar was a sprawling brick institution situated on the sea about a mile and a half from Portsmouth, where Atlantic storms frequently buffeted the coast and the massive ships of the British fleet would rendezvous. The huge three-storey hospital was an "immense pile of brick buildings," according to William Barton, a visiting naval surgeon and later first surgeon general of the United States Navy. It was dominated by a "grand front and two wings of great extent running at right angles from the front, forming a very spacious area within. In the center of this area is a chapel, a neat and appropriate building." Numerous large outbuildings dotted the extensive grounds, including workhouses and storerooms and several manses for the officers of the hospital. The thirty-two surrounding acres were hemmed in by a twelve-foot-high brick wall, making it look from the outside more like a prison than a place of healing. The walls were not to keep people out but to keep the patients in—in fact, to prevent them from deserting the Royal Navy. If given a chance, many sailors would escape as soon as they set foot ashore, fleeing to loved ones or to the grog shops in nearby Portsmouth.

Haslar was the largest and newest hospital in all of England, and probably the largest hospital in Europe. Constructed at great expense between 1754 and 1762, it could at full capacity comfortably hold as many as 2,500 patients and employed about 150 staff. Despite its formidable outer appearance, however, it was not a grim and unsanitary bunker. For its time, the hospital was a thoroughly modern, clean, and professional institution, with highly trained staff and a large annual operating budget. The hospital cost about £100,000 to build, an astonishing sum equivalent to the cost of constructing three of the largest battleships. The annual operating budget was around £20,000, a large sum in those days, when Lind earned the enviable salary of about £200 per year and a respectable house could be rented for around £40 per year. The British government had made a significant and remarkable investment in the hospital, a medical and financial commitment to the navy's sailors once

James Lind (1716–1794) conducted the first controlled trial in medical history as a lowly naval surgeon researching scurvy aboard the HMS *Salisbury* in 1747.

they had been brought ashore that seemed grand and excessive compared with their treatment aboard ship. Haslar was one of the great public works of the period.

The hospital was divided into numerous large wards capable of holding sixteen patients each, with a full five feet between their beds. For any wounded or sick mariner lucky enough to be brought here, it was a significant improvement over the dim, fetid, and airless compartments that passed as sick bays aboard ships. And despite the occasional nurse caught smuggling spirits to the sailors or persuading them to write wills in her favour, the medical and nursing staff were on a higher plane of professional competence than that generally found aboard ships, not to mention what the sailors could afford privately. At Haslar the convalescent sailors enjoyed comparatively spacious and clean wards, and the surgical and fever wards were also separated—an enlightened attempt by Lind to prevent cross-infection and the spread of disease. In the fever wards, sailors lay sweating and insensible, wasting away from yellow fever, dysentery, or malaria caught on voyages to distant shores. Fevers were so common in that day and age that perhaps a third of Haslar's patients were recovering from fevers at any given time.

Usually there were few men in the surgical wards, although after battles (quite frequent for the Channel fleet during the eighteenth century) great numbers of sailors could be bandaged and unconscious, recovering from serious wounds. Scorbutic sailors generally occupied about a third of Haslar's wards, and for brief periods they filled nearly the entire hospital. On any given day, ships could put into Portsmouth and discharge hundreds of scorbutic patients. Lind treated three to four hundred scorbutic sailors per day during the Seven Years' War and the War of American Independence, and occasionally double or triple that number.

Haslar hospital was admirably situated to receive the sick mariners. After disembarking from the ferries, sailors were conveyed to Haslar's receiving room by a water-carriage running in a narrow canal that led from the Spithead road through the gates to a small outbuilding, where they were bathed in hot soapy water and provided with clean clothing for the duration of their stay. Their filthy rags were taken to a nearby brick building and fumigated with burning pitch in an effort to rid them of lice and contagion. "We are remarkably clean," Lind wrote in a letter to a colleague. "No patient is admitted into the hospital until he is stripped of all his cloths and well washed with warm water and soap in tubs always kept for the purpose, he is allowed the hospital dress during the time he continues in the hospital or until his cloths are returned him quite clean, and he is regularly shifted and kept quite neat, clean and sweet at the Government's expense." When a fleet put into Portsmouth with a scorbutic outbreak, the debilitated men created a serious backlog in the admitting room. Many were billeted in tents on the hospital grounds.

Admitting this many scurvy patients on short notice was a huge logistical challenge. Hundreds of medical personnel rushed about the hospital, reorganizing beds, shifting the other patients into separate wards, and settling the newly arrived mariners in special scurvy wards. While ninety nurses kept the floors scrubbed and fumigated the wards to expunge any lingering foul vapours, purchasing agents rushed to town to arrange for fresh food for the new arrivals. Twenty-four local washerwomen were engaged to cleanse the sailors' filthy rags and bedding, smoking them with burning brimstone in the outbuildings or burning them if they were beyond repair. Cooks were roused, clergy were called to minister to the dying, and leave was cancelled for all the doctors and nurses. The patients were hastily placed on an antiscorbutic regimen of dietary supplements and other treatments believed to be beneficial. Curing scurvy in the hospital was costing the Admiralty a vast sum of money, but it was an unavoidable expense when the threat of invasion from France and Spain required the Channel fleet to be at sea as long as mariners' health held out.

The patients came and went by the hundreds, and as chief physician Lind was kept busy. Unfortunately, managing Haslar hospital proved to be a great deal of work and responsibility, and it consumed much of Lind's time and energy, leaving little room for him to continue his research into scurvy even while seeing its ravages daily. In the 1760s, Lind was also writing a third groundbreaking work, *Essay on Diseases Incidental to Europeans in Hot Climates, with the Method of Preventing Their Fatal Consequences.* It was published in 1768 and eventually ran through at least six editions. In it, Lind described the symptoms of many of the most common fevers that affected crews in tropical climates, such as the Black Vomit, the Bloody Flux, and the Dry Belly Ache, and gave suggestions on how to prevent and treat them. To prevent malaria, Lind advised captains to forbid men from sleeping ashore near stagnant water, to avoid contact with bad air. This would have been an effective preventative, but Lind recommended it for the wrong reason—it was the mosquitoes living in the swamp that carried the sickness, not the stagnant air itself. Lind's book remained the standard work on tropical medicine in the English language for fifty years. His suggestions for naval hygiene published in the 1757 essay (which, if implemented, would have been of great benefit to sailors) and his essay on tropical diseases (in itself a great contribution) established Lind as one of the great medical writers of the eighteenth century.

Unfortunately, throughout this time, Lind's thoughts on scurvy became ever more muddled. At Haslar, his job as chief physician was not to study scorbutic patients and conduct experiments but to return them to active duty as quickly as possible. The few trials he had the time to conduct produced variable, inconclusive, and occasionally contradictory results. He never reproduced a clinical trial like the one he ran aboard the *Salisbury*, and his conclusions never attained the same clarity.

After the publication of the first edition of the treatise in 1753, Lind became obsessed with concentrating citrus juice to make it more practical. A small dose of concentrated medicine given by the spoonful out of a bottle seemed more valid and dignified to the medical community than drinking a glass of fruit juice, and on ships that were already crammed with sailors and supplies, storing dozens of barrels of citrus juice was not ideal. Lemons and oranges were expensive and bulky, and the logistics of maintaining a national supply of fruit that had to be imported from the Mediterranean were complicated. Furthermore, fresh lemons could not survive at sea for months at a time any more than fresh broccoli or apples.

Lind developed a way of evaporating the water from fresh juice to create a concentrate that could be more easily stored aboard ships. He proposed "a method for preserving their [lemons and oranges] virtues entire for years in a convenient and small bulk . . . as oranges and lemons are liable to spoil and cannot be obtained at every port, nor at all seasons in equal plenty." He provided detailed instructions for the preparation of this "inspissated" juice, or "rob." He advised surgeons to pour the strained juice into a wide-mouthed bowl (to "favour evaporation") or "a common earthen basin used for washing, if well glazed," and to place the container into a pan of boiling water. The fruit liquid was to be kept just below boiling until sufficient water was evaporated, leaving the concentrate the "consistency of oil." It was then poured into small vials and corked for storage. "Thus the acid," he wrote, "and virtues of twelve dozen lemons or oranges, may be put into a quart-bottle, and preserved for several years."

Lind failed to test his rob, in spite of his pledge in the original edition of the treatise to "propose nothing dictated merely from theory; but shall confirm all by experience and facts, the surest and most unerring guides." If he had held true to this objective, it might not have taken several more decades for the Admiralty to implement an effective scurvy cure. Unfortunately, Lind was tricked by the fickle nature of the key ingredient, ascorbic acid, and his attempts to preserve fruits and vegetables by pickling, evaporation, or boiling destroyed the antiscorbutic properties that existed before preservation.

In the third edition of his treatise, Lind recommended as antiscorbutic numerous foods such as gooseberries, beer, and other fermented liquors such as cider, for which he provided no experimental justification whatsoever. "Green gooseberries," he claimed, "will keep for years, if, after being put into dry bottles their moisture is exhaled by putting the bottles slightly corked into a pot of water, which is allowed to come nearly to boil." Indeed this is true, but because Lind had no idea that ascorbic acid would be destroyed by heating, he assumed that if gooseberries remained edible and tasted fine, then they would remain antiscorbutic. Obviously he didn't test this assumption. In a 1951 experiment published in the journal *Medical History*, R. E. Hughes showed that although fresh gooseberries have about 50 to 65 milligrams per 100 millilitres of ascorbic acid (slightly higher even than fresh lemon juice), the ascorbic acid content was virtually nil after heating and bottling and about a month of storage. The same approximate level of decline is also evident in spruce beer, or fermented spruce tips. Fermentation actually eliminated the bulk of the ascorbic acid, while storage for several weeks took care of the rest.

Although Lind's concentrated lemon rob was very high in ascorbic acid when fresh, at about 240 milligrams per 100 millilitres, it had lost 50 percent of the ascorbic acid of the original lemons used to create it. That is to say, the same quantity of lemons before being made into a rob would have contained nearly 500 milligrams per 100 millilitres. After about a month of storage, 87 percent of the ascorbic acid had vanished, leaving the concentrate with about the same content as one regular fresh lemon. Although the rob was still a decent source of ascorbic acid, it was issued only in small doses because it was believed to have antiscorbutic powers ten times as great as the fluid by volume. Lind's rob was a very inefficient use of lemon juice, considering the cost of lemons and the effort involved in making it. The level of ascorbic acid in any given batch of rob could also vary wildly depending on the age and the amount of heat used in its preparation. If an inattentive physician or surgeon allowed the concentrate to boil, virtually all the vitamin C was lost. Lind also later learned that using glazed vessels to prepare the rob created a potentially poisonous concoction—the citrus juice absorbed lead from the glaze in hazardous quantities.

Without doing an empirical test on the rob's effectiveness, Lind would have had no logical reason to presume that creating the rob would have been detrimental to the "special" property of the acid. The concentrate looked fine, tasted fine, and was still acidic, so he surmised that it was still effective. Lind could never make the logical leap to understand why the special antiscorbutic property of a food should disappear after time or treatment—probably because he skipped a thorough test of this very hypothesis. A simple test would have revealed this flaw and taken one of the great mysteries out of his equation, leading him to a firmer conclusion of the curative powers of fresh citrus juice and perhaps an earlier or better understanding of scurvy. Lind had a difficult time convincing anyone to use his concentrated rob, however, even on navy-sponsored voyages to test various antiscorbutics, because it was very expensive and time-consuming to manufacture.

By the 1760s, there was an uneasy consensus amongst naval medical professionals that many of the time-honoured scurvy cures, such as smearing mercury paste on the open sores, consuming sulphuric acid as a dietary supplement, putting hydrochloric acid in the drinking water, and even the granddaddy of universal panaceas, bloodletting, were not contributing anything positive to the debate. The problems in the Royal Navy caused by scurvy, on the other hand, were if anything becoming more severe. Since the time of Anson's voyage in the 1740s, the incidence of scurvy aboard ocean-going ships had been increasing. Ships were spending an ever-greater time at sea, in distant and possibly hostile lands, while naval strategy increasingly involved patrolling foreign coasts. Ships were becoming larger, tours of duty longer, the demand for sailors greater. In 1764—after several decades that saw the publication of numerous treatises, tracts, essays, and proclamations on scurvy, its causes, and its cures, and several inconclusive experiments at the naval hospitals in Plymouth and at Haslar—the British Admiralty proposed to test antiscorbutics at sea, where no non-nautical influences might taint the outcome. The Seven Years' War with France had just ended, and the Admiralty had time to spare on non-military matters. The trial was an effort to acquire some reliable information on scurvy by sifting through the vast number of conflicting claims and suggestions.

The Admiralty commissioned John Byron to command a ship to do some preliminary exploration in the South Pacific while monitoring the effects of fresh provisions on the incidence of scurvy in his crew. It proved to be a short voyage—returning in under two years, in April 1766—and Byron's conclusions regarding antiscorbutics were sketchy and unreliable. The men had suffered terrible ravages from the disease, but owing to the Admiralty's instructions for Byron to purchase and outfit the ship with fresh vegetables whenever convenient, there were not a large number of deaths. Byron ordered scurvy grass and coconuts for his men, and while he claimed that the scurvy grass was of "infinite service" it was the coconuts that saved them from certain death. "It is astonishing the effect these nuts alone had on those afflicted. . . . Many in the most violent pain imaginable . . . and thought to be in the last stage of that disorder, were in a few days by eating those nuts (tho' at sea) so far relieved as to do their duty, and even to go aloft as well as they had done before." For the return voyage, Byron stocked up on more than two thousand coconuts and kept scurvy blessedly at bay. Byron's unscientific opinion that coconuts were a useful antiscorbutic was of little practical value to the Admiralty, however, as coconuts were not readily available in England. All in all, it was not a very illuminating trial.

A second voyage was hastily organized, this time specifically to test certain items that were thought to have the greatest antiscorbutic effect. Within a few months of Byron's return in the spring of 1766, two ships under the overall command of Samuel Wallis were outfitted and provisioned for an August sailing. Lind's rob was again not one of the antiscorbutic remedies to be evaluated—it was too expensive and its effectiveness was in question. The Sick and Hurt Board wrote to Lind in 1767 to express their doubts that citrus rob would be of use, since their own tests had proved equivocal, and they pointedly highlighted its expense and the impracticality of furnishing it in sufficient quantities to satisfy the navy. After the death of Lord Anson in 1762, Lind had no influential patron in the upper echelons of society to champion his cause and ideas. Although he was convinced of the value of his rob of oranges and lemons in combating scurvy, a new theory was on the ascendancy, and this one placed no stock in expensive citrus concentrates.

David MacBride was a Dublin physician who had served at sea briefly and was thirty-eight years old, ten years younger than Lind, when he wrote a medical tract titled *Experimental Essays* in 1764. He was a prime proponent of the putrefaction/fermentation theory of scurvy, which had been gaining in popularity throughout the mid-eighteenth century. The fashionable theory was based on ideas originally presented to the Royal Society by the Scottish physician Sir John Pringle in the 1750s. Pringle had been studying which substances either sped up or slowed down the putrefaction, or decomposition, of meats that were submerged in warm water. He discovered that fermenting bread seemed to significantly slow down the process. Based on Hermann Boerhaave's theory that scurvy was a "putrid disease" (with which even Lind agreed, claiming in the first and second editions of his treatise that it was blocked perspiration that caused the "putrefaction" in scurvy), anything that could delay, hinder, or prevent putrefaction was believed to be a strong candidate for countering the progression of scurvy. Pringle himself felt that sugar might even be an effective defence against putrid diseases because it stimulated fermentation.

MacBride's theory on scurvy was based on the premise that all living bodies have a certain quantity of "fixed air" within them. When bodies become putrefied or decomposed, a gas is released, which he believed was the fixed air escaping once it was no longer trapped within the living creature. Since all creatures release this gas, or fixed air, when they decompose, MacBride reasoned that the fixed air must be the binding agent for all living creatures. Fermentation would inhibit putrefaction because it created more fixed air, which then replaced the air that escaped during putrefaction or decomposition. Following this somewhat peculiar line of reasoning, a food that was easily fermented during digestion would be ideal for curing putrid diseases such as scurvy and tuberculosis. Malt of barley, MacBride felt, would be the most suitable substance for use by mariners since it was cheap, could be preserved for great periods of time, and could be quickly fermented into "sweet wort" whenever scurvy appeared in a crew. MacBride believed that with a regimen of several pints a day of the fermenting wort, scurvy would retreat because the body's supply of fixed air would be replenished. Wort of malt, MacBride proclaimed, "is to the full as powerful with respect to antiscorbutic virtue as the fresh juice of the acid fruits."

MacBride, taking Pringle's experiments with meat one step further, made the remarkable claim that he had prevented the putrefaction of meat by exposing it to fixed air in a bottle. He claimed also to have halted putrefaction by smothering meat in suet, thereby preventing the fixed air from escaping. MacBride also argued that fresh greens and fruits were antiscorbutic simply because they fermented easily during digestion; the standard seamen's ration of salt meat and biscuit was theoretically difficult to digest. In 1764 sweet wort was tested in the Royal Naval Hospital at Plymouth, but it showed no beneficial effects on the scorbutic sailors despite being issued in copious quantities. After one of the test patients wasted away and died, the others rebelled and refused to continue with the trial, claiming that "the wort produced very bad effects." Lind also conducted a two-week trial of the sweet wort at Haslar around the same time, and he too reported, not surprisingly, that it did little to halt the progression of scurvy. MacBride, whom the medical historian Sir James Watt has described as "a physician in search of a reputation," attributed the failure of these experiments not to his own ill-founded and self-serving theories but to the closed-minded nature of the Royal Navy (and presumably naval physicians). The failure, he wrote, "may easily be accounted for from that aversion to innovation and experiment which is so prevalent among mankind, but especially among seamen." MacBride later had his wort tested by the surgeon aboard his brother's ship, and the surgeon reported that it cured scurvy during the voyage. The wort of malt was rich in B-complex vitamins, which would have improved the nutritional content of the sailors' diet and reduced the incidence of beriberi and night blindness, but anyone who reported that the wort had beneficial effects on scurvy patients was either deluded or lying. Modern research has shown that wort made from fermented malt actually contains almost no vitamin C. "More trials we certainly shall have," MacBride announced, "now that the ice is fairly broken."

When Wallis returned from the Pacific with his report on the effectiveness of various antiscorbutics in 1768, he was vague and inconclusive about the benefits of MacBride's wort. The other substances he tested were portable soup and saloup (a mild, greasy beverage made from orchid roots and sauerkraut). Although scurvy was rampant on both of the ships, the antiscorbutic remedies were issued on an as-needed basis, and fresh food was eaten whenever the ships put in to shore. Wallis and the commander on the second ship, Philip Carteret, had no scientific or medical training, so their reports did not clarify which, if any, of the Admiralty's substances were beneficial against scurvy.

Lind never wavered in his belief that the stress of a naval life increased scurvy's hold upon men, and that lemon juice was the best antiscorbutic he had tested throughout his career. "To what has been said of the virtues of oranges and lemons in this disease, I have now to add, that in seemingly the most desperate cases, the most quick and sensible relief was obtained from lemon juice; by which I have relieved many hundred patients, labouring under almost intolerable pain and affliction from this disease, when no other remedy seemed to avail." It seems that Lind gave his patients at Haslar the fresh juice and created the rob for use on ships, and that he failed to test the rob at Haslar because he needed to cure the men as quickly as possible and had no time to create and experiment. Perhaps, too, Lind so strongly wanted the rob to be useful that he became blinded to its defects, since his friend and colleague Dr. Edward Ives had also found the rob "inferior to stored fruit juice" in his own personal tests. Yet Lind, unlike other contemporary physicians then writing about scurvy, did not deliberately conceal evidence that ran counter to his own theories and observations; if something didn't work and he knew of it, he included the information in the treatise.

Lind was fifty-six years old in 1772 when the third and final edition of his treatise was published. Overworked and increasingly dispirited from the results of his decades-long quest to understand scurvy, he seems to have given up hope of ever unravelling its mystery. "I carry my researches no further," he wrote. "A work, indeed, more perfect, and remedies more absolutely certain might have been expected . . . but, though a few partial facts and observations may, for a while, flatter with hopes of greater success, yet more enlarged experience must ever evince the fallacy of all positive assertions in the healing art." Although the third edition of the treatise was well received, and was published in French, Spanish, and Dutch, Lind seems to have admitted defeat and left off pursuing any further scurvy research. So close to a solution in his younger years, he lost the vigour to continue his research in a meaningful way as he neared retirement, and he also lost the energy or disposition to advocate for his early findings. Although he knew that fresh greens and citrus fruits could cure the affliction, he never concluded that the lack of them might be the cause of it. He never believed that scurvy was a deficiency disease, and he could never understand why fresh greens and citrus fruits should be beneficial, except that they were more easily digested than salt meat and hardtack.

In one instance, Lind went so far as to criticize the one person who had come to the conclusion that scurvy was a deficiency disease. "Others again," he wrote in the final edition of the treatise, referring to Johan Friedrich Bachstrom, the one theorist who truly understood scurvy, "have supposed such to be the constitution of the human body, that health and life cannot be preserved long, without the use of green herbage, vegetables, and fruits; and that a long abstinence from these, is alone the cause of the disease." Lind disputed that scurvy was caused directly by diet and cited several examples where scurvy apparently ran rampant despite the sailors' consuming fresh vegetables. "Upon a daily comparison of the state of those patients," he wrote, "I was surprised to find them all recovering pretty much alike, and though they abstained altogether from vegetables, yet they in general grew better." He concluded that "the disease would often, from various circumstances, take a favourable turn, which cannot be ascribed to any diet, medicine, or regimen whatever."

Although Lind never lost his desire to ameliorate the suffering of sailors in the navy, he had taken his understanding of scurvy as far as he could. His thinking had become muddled and his cherished early notions had been disproved by his own observations. He also became convinced that his early belief that scurvy had to do with the body's putrefaction was wrong or misleading. His experiments accurately showed that scorbutic patients were in no greater state of putrefaction than non-scorbutic patients (their blood or tissue had not actually decomposed, even at the height of the scorbutic symptoms). Lind's observations on putrefaction should have put a damper on Pringle's and MacBride's theories as well, but in the 1770s the idea that wort was an agent for counteracting the putrefying aspects of scurvy was gaining respect, helped greatly by the influence and stature of Pringle, who by 1772 was the president of the Royal Society.

The support for wort of malt as an antiscorbutic must have disillusioned Lind even further. He strongly suspected that the great idea that was being heralded as the best hope for a scurvy cure was false, and yet his own dear rob seemed equally ineffectual, perhaps making him second-guess the results of his original clinical trial from twenty-five years earlier. It must have been a bitter time for him. Eventually, a few years before his retirement, he went so far as to recommend as a scurvy deterrent cream of tartar—a substance he had already proved to be of no effect whatsoever. Lind had come full circle, and he ended up less clear on scurvy than when he was a lowly surgeon aboard the *Salisbury*.

But this failure to conduct rigorous and accurate scientific experimentation should be viewed less as a blemish on Lind's character than a sign that he was a product of his time. Lind could no more escape entirely the fashion in medicine and science than he could the fashion in clothing, writing, or politics. He was such a perceptive individual that he knew it. "It is perhaps the vain and chimerical belief of the existence of a never failing remedy for most diseases," he wrote, ". . . which has rendered the art of healing as variable and unconstant, as our dresses." Because of lack of communication, it was difficult for even informed members of the scientific community to trust each other's findings. There were no reliable or trustworthy peer-reviewed journals, no conferences, and few attempts to empirically prove theories. In the eighteenth century, there were no standards by which information could be accepted or verified other than by reproducing the experiment oneself—and without an accepted standard for experimental design, it was nearly impossible to conduct experiments that would yield meaningful results. Influential contacts had the greatest effect on a theory's acceptance.

Lind was never elected to the Royal Society, though many men of much lesser ability and accomplishments were readily admitted. Lind received no other honours in England during his lifetime, although he was elected to the French Royal Society of Medicine in 1776. He was prevented from achieving distinction within the scientific establishment because of his outspoken criticism of influential colleagues and his mediocre social standing. When he retired from Haslar in 1783 at the age of sixty-seven, it was with little fanfare, though his son, John, was allowed to succeed him in the lucrative position. Because he never wrote a memoir, little information exists about his personal life. Presumably he enjoyed a retirement free from financial worry with a pension of £200 per year. He died at Gosport in 1794 at the age of seventy-eight, three years before his wife.

Perhaps Lind's greatest professional accomplishment was that he inspired a generation of disciples, such as the future physician to the Channel fleet Thomas Trotter, James Cook, and the young Gilbert Blane. Although Lind never completely unbound the complex knot of scurvy, he set others onto the path that would see it virtually eliminated in the Royal Navy. Lind was a researcher, not an advocate. During the course of his life, he did not write a single essay, article, tract, or book devoted to publicizing his ideas. Refusing to be drawn into the battle, he never responded to public criticisms of his work by other physicians, instead merely plodding along revising his texts for the next edition. He was not interested in being the standard-bearer for an assault on contemporary naval and medical practices, or he feared that vocal criticism of his superiors in the navy might endanger his appointment at Haslar. His character can be best summed up by one of his own statements: "The Province has been mine to deliver Precepts: the Power is in others to Execute."

In Lind's defence, the theories and recommendations of individual physicians or surgeons could have had little positive effect in the eighteenth century. Although his *Salisbury* clinical trial was truly revolutionary, and his suggested cure for scurvy was more accurate than those of any of his contemporaries, Lind's advice alone would have been of little impact even had it been completely effective. To eliminate scurvy in the navy, an institutional revolution was needed. Merely providing evidence of an effective cure was not enough. The vast majority of ships that were large enough to be sailing on long voyages, or that had missions that kept them from port for extended periods of time, were owned and run by the government. This was true not only in England but in France, Spain, and Holland as well. The provisioning of these ships was organized by centralized victualling boards. So long as the standard, centrally purchased naval rations remained of poor nutritional content and quality, and entirely lacked in foods containing ascorbic acid, scurvy could never be cured on a meaningful scale.

The upper echelons of the naval establishment—people with busy schedules who were constantly bombarded with outlandish suggestions on all manner of naval matters (from victualling to the calculation of longitude to ship design) and whose attention was frequently diverted by wars, trade disputes, and other political considerations—had somehow to be persuaded. It was not an easy task even for someone with the proper connections and political clout, let alone for an obscure naval surgeon squarely from the middle classes, whose practical solutions were contradicted by other contemporary medical men and whose philosophical theorizing was as obtuse and bewildering as anything written in the eighteenth century. Naval surgeons and physicians pushing for a scurvy cure were like peeping mice in the corner of a great audience chamber—the decision makers could barely hear them and certainly could not understand their language.

But by the late 1760s, there was an awful lot of peeping vying for the Admiralty's attention. The benefits of solving the greatest medical mystery of the era could not only secure a reputation and a career but also, if the invention could be patented, make a man fabulously rich. It was becoming evident that scurvy was not caused by poor ventilation or damp air inhibiting natural perspiration. Nor was it caused by contagion or a blockage of the spleen. The potential cure that had the greatest institutional clout, and the support of the Royal Society, was MacBride's wort. It satisfied all the other required criteria admirably: it was portable; it could easily be stored shipboard for more than a year, and perhaps indefinitely; it wasn't overly bulky before being reconstituted; it didn't require too much fresh water, and fresh water was a rare commodity at sea; and most important, it was readily available at reasonable cost. But did it actually work? That had certainly been the great problem with other scurvy cures considered by the Admiralty. Although the first experimental voyages had proved inconclusive, the negative results had been vocally dismissed by MacBride, and Sir John Pringle remained convinced of wort's potential.

The members of the Admiralty board, perhaps disappointed with the results from their two previous ad hoc antiscorbutic trials, began planning a trial that would be more comprehensive and compelling; they were looking for a captain whose temperament would prove more thorough than that of Wallis or Carteret and whose conclusions would therefore be more persuasive. It would also have to be a voyage that wasn't dominated by an overriding and potentially vital military objective. The Admiralty certainly didn't think they could make a decision or advise the victualling board based on the scattered and distracted reports they had read, and another trial gave the appearance of their doing something to address the problem without the difficulty responsibility of making an expensive or potentially embarrassing decision. Fortunately, England was not at war between 1764 and 1775, and the immediate pressure was taken off the Royal Navy, reducing the length of time ships spent at sea and therefore the incidence of scurvy. Early in 1768, the Royal Society proposed a joint mission with the Royal Navy to the South Pacific, and a young, scientifically minded ship's master named James Cook was promoted to lieutenant and chosen as the commander. The objectives of the mission were threefold: the discovery of new lands, the recording of celestial phenomena, and, perhaps most significantly, the rigorous testing of a wide array of antiscorbutics.

7

MASTER MARINER: JAMES COOK'S GREAT VOYAGES IN THE PACIFIC

JUNE 3, 1769, was a languid and humid day on the small Pacific Island of Tahiti. "Not a cloud was to be seen the whole day," wrote Lieutenant James Cook, the commander of the expedition, "and the air was perfectly clear." While the ship *Endeavour* lay anchored offshore in a sheltered bay, a cluster of English officers and scientists eagerly drew near to the telescope that had been erected within the confines of a primitive fort. Two other telescopes had also been set up on the island to take independent observations of a celestial occurrence of great scientific importance. Quadrants were readied, ledgers opened, and smoked glass held before eyes. All waited with tension until 9:25 a.m., when the "whole of the planet Venus" began to slide across the face of the sun like a shadow.

For this they had sailed around the world from England the previous fall, and it was a great disappointment when they "very distinctly saw an atmosphere or dusky shade round the body of the planet which very much disturbed the times of the contacts . . . and we differed from one another in observing the times of the contacts much more than could be expected." The calculations would be imprecise. How could they record an accurate time of the eclipse when the fringe of the planet appeared hazy and indistinct? The observation of the transit of Venus was a component of the Royal Society's attempts to compute the distance between the earth and the sun, and it was one of the motivations for the Royal Navy's sending an expedition to the South Pacific. More significant than the observation of the transit of Venus, however, was that none of the men on the voyage—officers, scientists, or crew—had been seriously afflicted with scurvy in the ten months since they'd departed England. It was an unheard-of accomplishment, but it was not an accident.

Before taking command of the *Endeavour* in August 1768, the forty-year-old Cook was a promising non-commissioned ship's master who, by virtue of his abilities and work ethic, had attracted the attention of the Admiralty. He was a fine navigator despite his rudimentary formal education and his humble beginnings as a Scottish migrant labourer's son. Tall and stern, with the common touch of command, he had earned a secure and profitable position captaining a stout coal-laden "collier bark" in the North Sea by the age of twenty-seven. But the steady and predictable was not for Cook. A quest for adventure and his seemingly insatiable curiosity drove him to renounce his private command, enlist as an able seaman in the notoriously inflexible and elitist British Royal Navy at the outbreak of the Seven Years' War, and begin a wild and meteoric ride that brought him international fame and universal respect.

Cook's rise to commissioned status was not easy. Although he advanced quickly through the ranks of non-commissioned officers, command eluded him. He fought the French when the British captured Quebec City from the French in 1759, charting the St.

Captain James Cook (1728–1779), England's master mariner, who proved that scurvy could be defeated on lengthy voyages.

Lawrence River for the fleet. He spent five summer seasons patiently surveying the jagged coastline of Newfoundland in the North Atlantic, and making astronomical observations of a solar eclipse and other celestial movements that he later presented to the Royal Society in London. In no small part because of his skill at navigation and his interest in scientific observation, he was finally commissioned as a lieutenant, thirteen years after he enlisted, and given command of his own ship for an expedition for which he was eminently qualified—scientific exploration in uncharted waters.

For his ship Cook had made an unusual request. Instead of the standard navy vessel, he asked for the *Earl of Pembroke*, an ungainly and inelegant Whitby collier of the sort he sailed before joining the navy. Many sneered at the squat, uninspiring vessel, claiming it was unsuitable for the Royal Navy, but Cook knew that its shallow draft would suit admirably for coasting close to uncharted shores. The four-year-old vessel was refitted with cannons, perhaps cleaned of coal dust, had its hull reinforced, and was renamed *Endeavour* to reflect its illustrious future. Although it was only ninety-eight feet long and twenty-nine feet wide, it had a large cargo capacity, ideal for storing the provisions and scientific instruments for the ninety-four explorers. The *Endeavour* was crowded—prime conditions, according to some medical theorists, for scurvy and other diseases to take hold.

During his tenure in the Royal Navy, Cook had seen sailors suffer the debilitating ravages of the affliction—the bleeding gums, wobbly teeth, anemic lethargy, and black splotches discolouring their limbs before they expired in agony. In 1757, twenty-nine men succumbed to scurvy aboard his ship *Pembroke* as it sailed the St. Lawrence. During each year of his naval service, scurvy had spread through the crew, not always fatally, but that made it no less frightening and debilitating. Appalled by the suffering and loss of life, and aware of how it sapped a crew's potential, Cook eagerly embraced the Admiralty's tactics to curtail scurvy on the *Endeavour*. From the moment the ship departed Deptford at the end of August 1768, he began a regimen of cleanliness, fresh air, and an antiscorbutic diet, which involved stopping for fresh vegetables and water whenever possible and having the shipboard naturalists identify the edible exotic plants on foreign coasts. As part of the Admiralty's continued quest to discover a cure for scurvy, the *Endeavour* had been stocked with a vast array of antiscorbutics, nearly everything that was then being seriously proposed in medical circles, including barrels of malt, sauerkraut, marmalade of carrots, mustard, saloup, portable soup, distilled water, and, kept under key by the young naturalist Joseph Banks, a small quantity of James Lind's expensive rob of lemons and oranges.

Lind was then working on the third edition of his treatise, but there is no record of whether the *Endeavour*'s library was stocked with a copy of an early edition of the revolutionary book, and no record of whether Joseph Banks had ever read it. The Admiralty was particularly eager that Cook should experiment with the fermented wort of malt, which if proved antiscorbutic would have been a cheap and simple solution to the scurvy problem. The influential Sir John Pringle, the soon-to-be president of the Royal Society and another sponsor of the voyage, was also favourably disposed towards wort of malt as a scurvy cure, since it agreed with his own personal theories. The Admiralty specially gave Cook a copy of David MacBride's *Experimental Essays* and informed him that there was "great reason to believe that malt made into wort may be of great benefit to seamen in scorbutic and other putrid diseases."

As soon as the shadow of Venus vanished from the face of the sun on June 3, 1769, Cook returned to the *Endeavour* and opened a sealed packet of secret orders. If he was surprised by the magnitude of his new task, he makes no mention of it—his orders were to search for a mysterious southern continent that theoretically lay in the uncharted expanse of the Pacific Ocean. A wealthy and influential Scottish armchair adventurer named Alexander Dalrymple, a self-proclaimed expert on the southern continent, had pronounced that its existence was beyond question. According to his maps, the most accurate of the day, the earth was unbalanced, and a continent "was wanting on the South of the Equator to counterpoise the land to the North, and to maintain the equilibrium necessary for the Earth's motion." The southern continent had to exist, he claimed, or surely the earth would have wobbled and spun out of control. The population of this new land he predicted to be fifty million people, and it was of "greater extent than the whole civilized part of Asia, from Turkey eastward to the extremity of China." Dalrymple imagined that the trade potential alone would be "sufficient to maintain the power, dominion and sovereignty of Britain, by employing all its manufactures and ships." If the southern continent existed, it would bring great wealth to the nation that first discovered it, and now that the transit of Venus had been duly observed, it was Cook's job to locate it.

England was not alone in searching for the magnificent landmass. In 1770 Don Manuel de Amat, viceroy of Peru, sent two ships to the vicinity of Tahiti and the South Pacific, but they failed to find the great southern continent. And a French expedition under Compte Louis Antoine de Bougainville had in 1768 also landed at Tahiti, the crew suffering horribly from scurvy, with spotted, weeping sores and agonizing joint pains. By the time they arrived, several mariners were already dead and others were so weakened they could barely go ashore. Bougainville later wrote that "people have long argued about the location of Hell. Frankly, we have discovered it." He was referring to his own ship, not the tropical paradise of Tahiti, where he was able to reprovision with fresh food and nurse his dying mariners back to health. Bougainville pressed on, hoping to discover something marvellous in the uncharted expanse of the South Pacific, but he and his mariners were soon suffering horribly once again. At the end of August 1768, Bougainville and his scorbutic and malnourished men were delivered from their despondent degeneration when they sighted a Dutch settlement on Buru Island, in Indonesia. "One must have been a sailor," he wrote, "and reduced to the extremities which we had felt for several months together, in order to form an idea of the sensation which the sight of greens and a good supper produced in people in that condition." Although many western European nations were scouring the seas for new lands, scurvy held them all in thrall.

Cook's new orders for the *Endeavour* were to put to sea "without loss of time," once Venus had finished its transit. For many of his men, leaving Tahiti would take stoic fortitude. It was not easy to bid farewell to what had been their tropical home for the past several months—two sailors had "strongly attached themselves" to the brown beauties of the island. But the navy was a harsh life, and they soon returned to their posts. While the ship made ready to depart, "the carpenters employed stocking the anchors and the seamen in getting the ship ready for sea," Cook made sure that as many local plants and fruits as they could stock were lowered into the hold.

As they swished out into the expanse of sea and sadly bade farewell to the lush island behind them, Cook turned his mind to the problem of the southern continent. It did not seem promising, despite the magnitude of the uncharted Pacific. Cook had always been skeptical of the existence of a great southern continent, and his suspicions were confirmed by a Tahitian priest named Tupaia who had come aboard the ship for the remainder of the voyage at Banks's urging. Although Tupaia claimed to have a great knowledge of the surrounding islands, and sketched several on a map, Cook prophetically observed that "we cannot find that he either knows or ever heard of a Continent." After passing a small archipelago of islands that Cook good-humouredly named the Society Islands because they "lay contiguous to each other," the *Endeavour* ploughed south into a seemingly endless sea of ruffled water shimmering in the sun.

By early September they had passed below the fortieth parallel, and Cook ordered the *Endeavour* to change course and head west. For another month they were greeted by nothing but sea and wind, with the occasional storm to break the monotony, and soon scurvy showed itself amongst the crew. Cook immediately ordered the anti-scorbutics to be brought forth from the sick bay, particularly the sauerkraut, and the scourge retreated. Banks treated his own early symptoms with Lind's rob of lemon and oranges, to immediate effect. By early October, mariners scanning the water spied bits of seaweed, bark, and birds—a sure sign of nearby land. From his rudimentary charts, Cook knew they were probably nearing New Zealand, an unexplored landmass first recorded on a map by the Dutch mariner and explorer Abel Tasman a century earlier.

In the rolling and pitching sea just off the eastern coast, Cook stood on the deck and strained to glimpse the land through the haze, but he could discern only patches of dark green forest and the crest of mountains peeking above the fog. The smell of smoke suggested the land was inhabited, and Banks wrote that "all hands seem to agree that this is certainly the continent we are in search of." As they sailed south, Cook kept his bobbing ship clear of the fearsome coast to avoid hidden shoals and sunken rocks. When they did finally put into a sheltered bay, their first contact with the local people ended in bloodshed when four Maoris attacked the water crew and were driven off with guns. Several more Maoris were shot when they attempted to steal muskets. After the friendly reception on Tahiti, the violence damped the spirit of the crew; Banks wrote, "Thus ended the most disagreeable day My life has yet seen, black be the mark for it and heaven send that such may never return to embitter future reflection."

Cook named the bay Poverty Bay, both "because it afforded us no one thing that we wanted," and because he feared sending a landing party ashore to collect greens despite his worries about an outbreak of scurvy. He spent the next six months cruising the New Zealand coastline, charting it to determine whether it was an extension of the fabled great southern continent. Relations with the Maoris remained unpredictable. On several occasions the *Endeavour* frightened advancing Maori war canoes with cannon fire, but on other occasions the mariners peacefully traded cloth and nails for wood and vegetables, including taro, yams, sweet potatoes, and hearts of palm—all very nutritious and antiscorbutic. The language of the Maoris was similar to that spoken on Tahiti, and Tupaia was able to translate basic information and questions.

Eager to free themselves from the confines of the crowded and stinking ship, Banks and the other naturalists took every opportunity to go ashore, collecting hundreds of new species of plants to be studied later—and to be eaten when scurvy reappeared. In addition to the wild grasses, roots, bulbs, and foreign fruits they collected, the *Endeavour* had aboard a complement of foods deemed antiscorbutic. The mess tables were frequently laden with trenchers of sloppy, fermenting cabbage blended with other tantalizing ingredients, such as wild celery, onions, or scurvy grass. "The Sour Krout the Men at first would not eate," noted Cook sagely in his journal, revealing one of his leadership secrets, "until I put in practice a Method I never once knew to fail with seamen, and this was to have some of it dress'd every Day for the Cabbin Table. . . . Whatever you give them out of the Common way, altho it be ever so much for their good yet it will not go down with them and you hear nothing but murmurings gainest the man that first invented it; but the Moment they see their Superiors set a Value upon it, it becomes the finest stuff in the World and the inventor a damn'd honest fellow." He also strictly forbade the ship's cook from serving the slush, the residual fat from the boiled salt pork and beef (and though this didn't actively deter scurvy, it certainly had other health benefits, such as preventing copper poisoning). Cook also encouraged and "enforced by example" cold baths, and he inspected the hands of mariners, punishing those who showed lack of cleanliness by restricting their grog.

Banks and Cook observed and wrote about the Maoris, their communities, foods, social customs, and population, even recording disturbing evidence of cannibalism. At one point Cook found himself trading in a community of Maoris who "not long before must have been regaling themselves upon human flesh, for I got from one of them a bone of the fore arm of a Man or Woman which was quite fresh, and the flesh had been but lately picked off, which they told us they had eat." It was the remains of a tribal enemy killed in a skirmish. Although Cook was offended, a woman assured him that they did not eat their own people, only their foes.

Because of Cook's rigid enforcement of diet and cleanliness, there were still ninety-one mariners to celebrate Christmas in 1769 (three had died, but not from scurvy). Spirits were high, and after shooting several wild geese and roasting them to perfection for a great feast, the sailors became, according to Banks, "as Drunk as our forefathers used to be upon the like occasion." They continued sailing in the New Year, and by mid-January Cook suspected that New Zealand consisted of two distinct islands. By April the *Endeavour* had circumnavigated both of them. "This country," Cook wrote, "which before now was thought to be part of the imaginary southern continent, consists of Two large islands." He duly took possession of the islands, in the standard manner of eighteenth-century discoverers, for "His Majesty King George III" before again setting sail for the west in mid-April.

The *Endeavour* was loaded with fresh local produce, the mariners were healthy, and in about two weeks, and before scurvy began to show, the lookout had spied land on the western horizon. Although Cook expected, from vague and unreliable Dutch reports, that some landmass lay to the south of Indonesia and the East Indies, no European had any idea of its size or dimensions. The land appeared disappointingly barren at first but soon became "woody and pleasant" as they coasted north. On April 28, 1770, the *Endeavour* glided into a peaceful bay and dropped anchor. Although Cook initially called the place Stingray Harbour, he later changed the name to Botany Bay, "from the great number of new plants collected there." Banks and the naturalists spent until May 6 hastily gathering all the new plants they could find from the nearby forest. One of the antiscorbutic plants Banks collected was a sort of leafy spinach he called *Tetragonia cornuta*—Botany Bay greens.

Restocked with plants and fruits, the *Endeavour* set off north along the coast, unknowingly entering the treacherous region of the Great Barrier Reef—a thousand-mile stretch of islands and jagged coral cliffs lying deceptively beneath the swirling waters. At night on Sunday, June 10, disaster struck. With a sickening crack, the *Endeavour* lurched to halt, the oaken hull gashed on a razor-sharp outcropping of coral. Cook rushed on deck as the ship jolted and began to fill with water. He immediately ordered nearly fifty tons of iron and stone ballast, spoiled provisions, and six massive cannons thrown overboard. It "seemed to be the only means we had left to get her off," he wrote.

The ship had struck at high water, and they spent a harrowing night stuck to the coral waiting for the next tide. The crew manned the three suction pumps, furiously trying to prevent the ship from foundering, and all available hands readied themselves to haul on the anchors and to row furiously from the small boats to drag the stricken *Endeavour* off the reef. They all knew it was certain death if they failed—in the morning light they could see the distant coast of Australia more than twenty miles away, and there were no islands nearby. As the tide rose, all hands heaved on the anchor lines and tow lines until, with another crack, the ship shuddered and slid away from the reef before settling into the water. It didn't immediately sink as Cook had feared; miraculously, a great chunk of the coral had lodged itself into the hole in the hull.

They further controlled the leaking by dragging a tar-soaked sail around the hull like a bandage, and then they began a slow journey to the unknown shore. Although it was an "alarming and I may say terrible Circumstance" that "threatened immediate destruction to us as soon as the Ship was afloat," the pumps held the water at bay for the next five days until the wounded *Endeavour* limped into the sheltered estuary of a river Cook later christened the Endeavour River. The vessel was careened in the secluded spot, and they spent the next seven weeks repairing the hull and exploring the brown, dry, and ill-looking land. Fortunately, giant turtles swam in the lagoons, kangaroos dwelt in the scrub, and antiscorbutic plants were abundant. Scurvy materialized in none of the men except for Tupaia, "whose bad gums were very soon followed by livid spots on his legs & every symptom of inveterate scurvy." But he was soon recovered after "living entirely on what he Caught."

After the carpenters had patched the hull as best they could, the *Endeavour* was launched and began a slow reconnaissance of the remainder of the east coast of Australia. At the end of August, they approached the northern tip of the continent, Cape York, and steered into the Torres Strait, the narrow strip of water separating Australia from New Guinea. Glancing back along the vast distance of coastline he had just sailed, and perhaps smelling the smoke from the fires of the people who lived there, Cook claimed it all for England and named it New South Wales. The name was changed to Australia when, several decades later, Britain began shipping convicts to the continent and establishing penal colonies.

The uncertainty of the voyage had passed—the waters of the East Indies were well known and well travelled. Cook put into harbour at the Dutch port of Batavia (now Jakarta), on the Indonesian island of Java, to pick up supplies and to repair the ship's hull more thoroughly for the return voyage. The grateful crew loaded up on mangoes, grapes, watermelons, tamarinds, and coconuts, as well as fresh beef, pork, and lamb. Unfortunately, the port was a stinking, unsanitary filth-hole teeming with mosquitoes from nearby swamps and stagnant canals, and the water was tainted and unclean. During two and a half months the crew spent repairing the ship and enjoying the pleasures of civilization in the unwholesome port, malaria and dysentery latched on to seventy-three of them, including Cook and Banks. In the first months Cook recorded, "we were so weakened by sickness that we could not muster above 20 men and officers that were able to do duty." Twenty-nine men, including Tupaia, perished from the diseases of Batavia before the *Endeavour* dropped anchor in England on June 12, 1771, and the weary mariners stepped onto their native soil after two years and nine and a half months at sea. But none had died from scurvy.

Cook's medical accomplishment was as astounding as his geographical one. Had he really conquered scurvy? If so, it would be a greater breakthrough than the discovery of Dalrymple's southern continent, a military and commercial advantage on par with the accurate calculation of longitude. No longer would the Admiralty have to budget for a 50 percent or higher death rate, which routinely jeopardized the success of expensive and sensitive missions around the globe. Certainly this voyage was a counterpoint to Anson's tremendous losses crossing the Pacific thirty years earlier.

Sadly, none of the measures used on Cook's voyages was put into effect on other ships at this time—the navy wanted irrefutable proof of a specific cure for the dreaded disease before changing its regulations, and there was always the possibility that Cook had merely been lucky. The fact that half his crew had died on the voyage obscured the astounding success of Cook's battle against scurvy. Lind released the pessimistic third and final edition of his treatise in

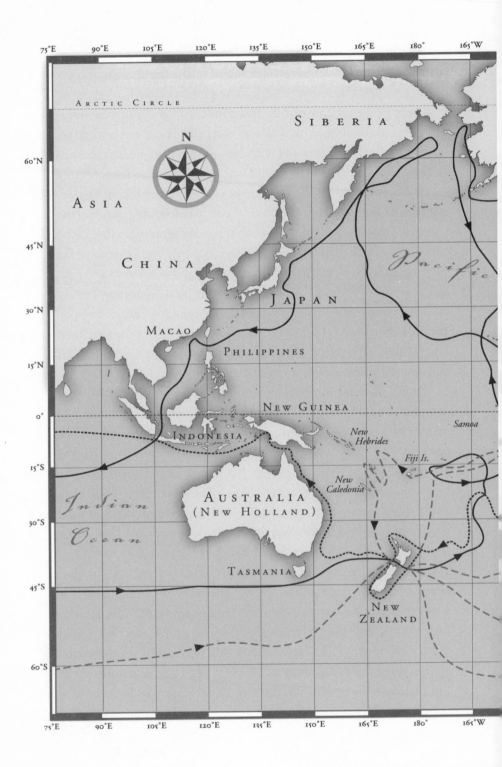

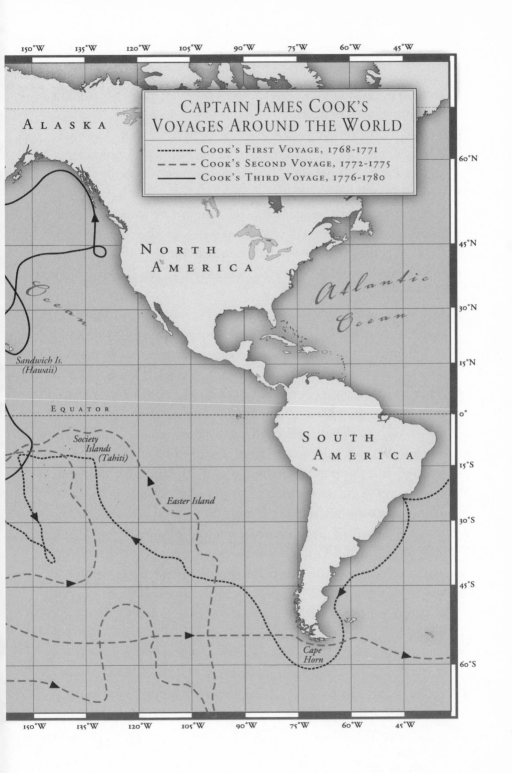

CAPTAIN JAMES COOK'S
VOYAGES AROUND THE WORLD

.... COOK'S FIRST VOYAGE, 1768-1771
— — — COOK'S SECOND VOYAGE, 1772-1775
———— COOK'S THIRD VOYAGE, 1776-1780

ALASKA

NORTH
AMERICA

Atlantic
Ocean

Ocean

Sandwich Is.
(Hawaii)

EQUATOR

Society
Islands
(Tahiti)

SOUTH
AMERICA

Easter Island

Cape
Horn

150°W   135°W   120°W   105°W   90°W   75°W   60°W   45°W

60°N

45°N

30°N

15°N

0°

15°S

30°S

45°S

60°S

1772, not long after Cook's return; the same year, Pringle was elevated to president of the Royal Society, bringing institutional clout in favour of wort of malt.

Despite the amazing distance Cook covered, the issue of a hidden continent had not yet been resolved to the Admiralty's satisfaction, and he was soon ordered to "Circumnavigate the Globe in a higher parallel than has hitherto been done." In other words, he was to search one of the last remaining blank spots on the planet—the seas surrounding the South Pole. Within a year and a half of his return, Cook was off again to sweep the South Seas, probe the fringes of the frightening, ice-bound Antarctic, and map the islands of Polynesia and New Zealand.

Owing to the proposed length of the voyage (perhaps three years), the victualling board was extremely eager to provide a full complement of antiscorbutics for continued testing, which was preferable to anyone's making a decision. Again Cook was urged to experiment with wort of malt (the Admiralty, heeding the persuasions of Pringle, truly hoped it would prove an effective antiscorbutic). Cook ordered, for each of his two hundred mariners, nearly one hundred pounds of sauerkraut, twenty-five pounds of salted cabbage, fifteen pounds of portable soup, thirty-one "half-barrels of malt and wort," in addition to a somewhat bewildering array of other antiscorbutics, including more "rob of oranges and lemons which we found of great use in preventing the scurvy from laying hold of our men." The rob was made by one of Lind's disciples, Nathaniel Hulme, who provided specific instructions on how it was to be used. At the Admiralty's suggestion and on the advice of Baron Storsch of Berlin, Cook also included thirty gallons of a carrot-marmalade paste. "A spoonful of this marmalade," Storsch wrote, "mixed with water and taken now and then will prevent the scurvy, it will even cure it if constantly taken." Also new for the voyage was a machine from Joseph Priestley for making "water impregnated with fixed air." This was in aid of a newly fashionable but fortunately short-lived variation of the fermentation theory that suggested that soda water would be an even more potent antiscorbutic than wort of malt for cleansing stale air from the body. Cook was willing to try even the most preposterous treatments if they held the slightest chance of saving the lives of his men.

Cook arranged for the purchase of two ships, the *Resolution* and the *Adventure*, both Whitby colliers and both lavishly outfitted with every modern convenience, including a new device for calculating longitude, a Harrison chronometer. The *Adventure* was commanded by Tobias Furneaux, a recently promoted lieutenant who had been in the South Pacific with Wallis in 1766. The vessels proudly set to sea in July 1772, and in three months they were harboured at the Cape of Good Hope, on the southern tip of Africa. While the men went ashore and gathered plants and fresh water for their dash towards Antarctica, two Dutch East India ships lumbered into port, having lost 150 men to scurvy during their four-month voyage from Holland.

On November 22, 1772, the *Resolution* and the *Adventure* hoisted sails and headed south to the Antarctic. It was early summer in the southern hemisphere. Initially, they were searching for a jutting pinnacle of the southern continent that had been reported by the French mariner Jean Bouvet de Lozier in 1739. Lozier had named the promontory Cape Circumcision, and he claimed to have clearly seen the icy mountains looming from the misty seas south of Africa. But as Cook's ships manoeuvred through the alternately rough and calm seas, they were halted by "an immense field of ice, to which we could see no end." The two ships turned east and began to follow the growling wall through an increasingly haunting landscape, with the surface of the water draped in mist that occasionally swirled apart to reveal distant islands and fantastic drifting ice castles. The fog seemed to consume all sound, yet sometimes they were startled by the spout of a distant whale or a cluster of curlews crying as they flew overhead.

Cook wrote that these "lands were doomed by nature to perpetual frigidness never to feel the warmth of the sun's ray; whose terrible and savage aspect I have not words to describe—such are the lands we have discovered." As they continued their polar circumnavigation, the two ships became lost in the fog and rough seas and did not meet up again until they rendezvoused at Queen Charlotte Sound, in New Zealand, three months later, on May 19, 1773.

In the intervening months the two ships had tracked the icy wastes alone. When Cook and the *Resolution* reached New Zealand after 117 continuous days at sea, he was pleased to note that "after such a long continuance at sea in a high southern latitude it is but reasonable to think that many of my people would be ill of the scurvy. The contrary, however, happened." Only one sailor was suffering from scurvy, and even his illness, Cook related, was "occasioned chiefly by a bad habit of body and a complication of other disorders." As a precaution, however, Cook ordered the brewing of spruce beer, a drink that Lind had written about in the first edition of his treatise, and that had apparently worked with surprising results for the Natives along the barren coast of Labrador. Cook used "the leaves and branches of a tree which resembles the American black spruce." All was not so well aboard the *Adventure*, however. Many of the men were debilitated and weakened from scurvy, but they soon recovered with the fresh greens collected in New Zealand.

After reprovisioning and taking on water, both ships set sail for Tahiti and the Society Islands to wait out the winter. Again the crew of the *Adventure* suffered from scurvy on the two-week voyage. When Cook "sent aboard the *Adventure* to enquire into the state of her crew, I learnt that her cook was dead and about twenty more were attacked" with the disease. "I do not know," he admitted, "how to account for the scurvy raging more on one ship than the other, unless it was owing to the crew of the *Adventure* being more scorbutic when they arrived at New Zealand than we were, and to their eating few or no vegetables while they lay in Queen Charlotte

Sound, partly because it was a new diet, which alone was sufficient for seamen to reject it." Either the captain of the *Adventure*, Furneaux, was not so diligent as Cook in overseeing the diet of his mariners or he lacked the diplomacy to convince them of the benefits of fresh food and antiscorbutics.

In July 1773, Cook took the drastic step of ordering Furneaux to follow Cook's own scurvy-fighting methods and change the diet of the crew. "To introduce any new article of food among seamen," Cook wrote, "let it be ever so much for their good, requires both the example and authority of a commander, without both of which, it will be dropped before the people are sensible to the benefits resulting from it. . . . There was hardly a man in the ship that did not attribute our being free of the scurvy to the beer and vegetables we made use of in New Zealand." Scurvy was reduced on the *Adventure* after Furneaux was admonished for his inattention to the welfare of his sailors.

For the next several years, Cook used New Zealand and Tahiti as bases while he sailed back and forth around Antarctica and the South Pacific, searching for the mysterious southern continent. Cook was ever vigilant, and he kept up his regimen of stopping for fresh foods and encouraged the surgeons to maintain a liberal dosage of all antiscorbutics at regular intervals. He didn't care what made the men healthy, so long as they remained able to carry out their duties. On one instance in mid-1774, Cook recorded in his journal that "although I must own, and that with pleasure, that on our arrival here [the Marquesas Islands] it could be hardly said that we had one sick man on board, and not above two or three who had the least complaint. This was undoubtedly owing to the many antiscorbutic articles we had on board and the great care and attention of the Surgeon who took special care to apply them in time."

When he triumphantly returned to England in July 1775, having spent nearly seven consecutive years exploring the far side of the globe without losing a single man to scurvy, Cook was the toast of

Europe. King George III awarded him a royal coat of arms, he was promoted to the rank of post captain, he visited the homes of great scientists and lords of the Admiralty, and he was elected a fellow of the Royal Society. Cook gave oratories on his scientific and navigational observations to learned societies, and he should have been contemplating retirement from his life on the sea. By virtue of his own nautical brilliance and determination, he had beaten England's rigid caste system, but he was unable to rest on his laurels.

When the forty-eight-year-old Cook was asked by the Admiralty if he could recommend a suitable captain for a high-profile voyage to one of the most inaccessible regions of North America, the Strait of Anian, or the Northwest Passage, he immediately turned down a lucrative retirement posting in charge of Greenwich Hospital and volunteered himself. Settling rumours about the Strait of Anian would be the pinnacle of his wildly successful career, a final glorious achievement that would secure his place as the greatest naval captain of his time.

The fabled Strait of Anian was the elusive waterway through North America that many in the British Admiralty believed held the key to global maritime dominance (because it would provide a shorter northern route to the Pacific Ocean and the Orient). The mythical strait could be anywhere—knowledge of the geography west of the Mississippi and the Great Lakes at this time was vague at best, and sometimes bordered on unfounded but optimistic speculation. Once again Cook would be sailing to prove something didn't exist. French charts showed a vast inland sea authoritatively occupying most of what is now the western United States, and the mariner Juan de Fuca claimed to have navigated the waterway through to the Atlantic Ocean for Spain two centuries earlier. The most recent Russian charts depicted Alaska as an island and showed a clear Pacific entrance to the "open" polar sea. Unravelling the great geographical mystery that had perplexed cartographers and explorers for centuries would be immensely satisfying to Cook, who many believed embodied the very ideals of eighteenth-century European intellectual and scientific achievement. Knowing that with Cook their chances of survival and fame were much improved, mariners and officers from throughout the country, and even from Europe, applied for positions aboard his ships. He was a busy man again preparing for a voyage that would depart less than a year after his return.

During and immediately following Cook's first and second voyages, scurvy continued to run rampant on other navy ships. However, it was obvious to even the most obtuse of naval bureaucrats that something Cook had done had prevented every single mariner from succumbing to the dreaded sea scourge during seven years at sea, and that it would be of great benefit to the Royal Navy if his feat could be repeated. Scurvy was still considered a disease (its symptoms were similar to other diseases), and its "cure" had to be cheap and easy to obtain—the navy wanted a solution that reflected the value of the life of the average sailor. And even as it became apparent that a ship operating with a vigorous and healthy crew was much more valuable than one operating at half strength, centuries of tradition and a complacent bureaucracy proved to be monumental obstacles to change.

What exactly needed to be done to eradicate scurvy was still debatable. The medical reports from Cook's first and second voyages were conflicting and ambiguous, leaving plenty of room for interpretation. Following the first voyage, Cook and his surgeon, William Perry, reported favourably on the antiscorbutic value of both citrus rob and wort of malt, yet they also reported that neither had any value. One part of Perry's report stated that a test of the wort was "almost entirely precluded" by the effectiveness of the citrus rob. He then wrote that "a trial was made of the robs and attended with success." However, Perry also claimed that wort of malt was frequently used, and he concluded that "from what I have seen the wort perform, from its mode of operation, from Mr.

MacBride's reasoning, I shall not hesitate a moment to declare my opinion, viz; that Malt is the best medicine I know, the inspissated Orange and Lemon juices not even excepted."

The journal of Sir Joseph Banks, the botanist and physician on Cook's first voyage and the successor to Sir John Pringle as head of the Royal Society, is also illuminating. Unfortunately, his journal was not published for more than a century, which kept out of public discourse information that would have been valuable to the debate on scurvy. Banks reported in his journal that although he drank "a pint or more" of wort each evening, he began to show signs of scurvy. "I then flew to the lemon juice . . ." he wrote. "Every kind of liquor which I used was made sour with the lemon juice, so that I took nearly 6 ounces a day of it; the effect of this was surprising, in less than a week my gums became firm as ever." The Admiralty had supplied him with only about twenty-four pints of the valuable elixir (as well as a small quantity of rob), so it was not generally issued to the crew except in small doses in extreme situations. Perhaps Banks reserved it for himself and the officers. Banks's report reveals his own suspicion that malt did little to fend off scurvy. Even more telling is that when scurvy did manifest itself, the first thing he turned to was the lemon juice and rob. Could Cook not have been aware of this? The two were on close terms and spent nearly three years together on a ship less than thirty feet wide and a hundred feet long. As a captain concerned with the well-being of his crew, Cook must have conferred with the ship's naturalist about the state of their health and indeed about Banks's own health.

Banks, however, later wrote in his journal on the apparent success of wort of malt as a scurvy cure. I "either received," he speculated, "or thought I received, great benefit from the use of this mess." He then explained why he thought the wort might have been effective. "For my own part I should be inclined to believe that the salubrious qualities of the wort which arise from fermentation might in some degrees at least be communicated to the wheat when thoroughly saturated with its particles, which would consequently acquire a virtue similar to fresh vegetables, the greatest resisters of sea-scurvy known." Banks, who apparently had read MacBride's *Experimental Essays*, was led to a tentative belief in the antiscorbutic properties of wort of malt because it made theoretical sense, even though earlier he had reported that scurvy crept up on him while he was drinking wort of malt daily. It appears that Banks was no more immune to the insidious lure of fashionable theory than others.

At the end of his second voyage, in 1775, Cook had no clearer idea of which antiscorbutics were the most effective. In the opinion of Cook and his surgeons, the soda water and saloup were completely useless, and the marmalade of carrots was never tried. The portable soup he found to be "exceedingly beneficial" because the cooks added to it fresh vegetables that the men otherwise would not have eaten. Cook also felt that "Oyle" in a sailor's diet promoted scurvy, and he suggested banning butter and cheese altogether. At the very least, he suggested, "ye Ships would be clear of that disagreeable Smell, caused by rotten cheese."

At one point he claimed that wort of malt "is without doubt one of the best antiscorbutic sea medicines yet discovered; and if used in time will, with proper attention to other things, I am persuaded, prevent the scurvy from making any great progress for a considerable while. But I am not altogether of opinion that it will cure it at sea. We have been a long time without any, without feeling the want of it, which might be owing to other articles." Christopher Lloyd and Jack Coulter point out in their 1961 work *Medicine and the Navy* that the last sentence was omitted from the printed edition of Cook's report, lessening the negative impact of his already tentative and qualified endorsement. When one of Cook's lieutenants informed him that scurvy had appeared in the crew despite the fact that they had been drinking daily doses of wort of malt, Cook sketched in his journal that "it would be proper to examine the Surgeon's journal to know when and in what quantity the wort was given to these scorbutic people, for if it was properly applied, we have a proof that it alone will neither cure nor prevent the sea-scurvy." For some reason, the examination of the surgeon's journal was either never done or never reported.

Cook was brief but clear about the effectiveness of citrus juice and rob on the second voyage. "The Surgeon made use of it in many cases with great success," he claimed. The surgeon, James Patten, however, failed to mention that he ever tested citrus juice or rob on the voyage. But in his official report, Patten praised wort of malt as "the best remedy hitherto found out for the cure of the sea scurvy. . . . I am well convinced, from what I have seen the wort perform, that if aided by portable soup, sauerkraut, sugar, sago and currants, the scurvy will seldom or never make its alarming presence amongst a ship's crew on the longest voyages." The evidence and opinions about rob and wort of malt were remarkably confused and contradictory.

Cook could offer only vague and unqualified opinions on the most effective antiscorbutics because he was not conducting controlled trials, like those organized by Lind, but was busy managing the expeditions. Preventing scurvy was only a sideshow, although it proved to be an important one, to his primary objective of geographical discovery. Different trials, by Cook and others, continued to return conflicting results because the trials themselves were never standardized or carried out with sufficient zeal. Nevertheless, it is a fitting reminder that the master mariner James Cook's most prestigious award, the Royal Society's Copley Gold Medal, was given not for his geographical discoveries or military victories but for his medical accomplishments.

Less than a year after returning from the limitless South Pacific, on July 4, 1776, two days after the Thirteen Colonies officially declared their independence from Britain, Cook embarked on his final voyage of discovery, to the mysterious hinterland of the American continent. Because of the scientific value of the voyage and

Cook's international fame, Benjamin Franklin requested that American privateers not hinder Cook's ships, and the French government later also agreed to let them pass freely. The *Resolution* and the smaller *Discovery*, with 191 mariners, cruised down the estuary at Portsmouth to the Atlantic. The two ships sailed three-quarters of the way around the globe (dipping south around Africa, winding through the Indian Ocean, stopping at Tahiti near the end of 1777, and landing for the first time in Hawaii on the way) before nearing the misty shore of Oregon on March 7, 1778, and heading north along the west coast of North America as far as the Bering Strait. No one suffered horribly from scurvy despite the many months at sea.

Fleeing the polar winds and the icy morass of the Arctic in the fall of 1778, the two ships quickly headed for the balmier Hawaiian climate, where the mariners settled in for a leisurely winter of feasting and carousing. Cook nevertheless vowed to return the following spring for a final foray into the frigid Bering Strait. But it was not to be. Cook had been showing signs of fatigue and weariness throughout the third voyage. He was occasionally ill and morose. His temper flared in circumstances where previously he would have remained calm. His violent outbursts towards his own crew and the Natives on various Pacific islands seem almost unreal, the behaviour of a more sinister or less caring man. The incidences of flogging were double those on his previous voyages. When an islander in the Tahiti region stole several goats, he ordered the man's hair shaved and his ears cut off.

The stresses of leading frightening and harrowing voyages, the expectations that had increased along with his fame, were beginning to take their toll. The *Resolution* was also in a bad state—leaking and poorly outfitted, the result of shoddy workmanship in England—and on one occasion Cook loudly and publicly cursed and swore at the navy board while stamping about the deck. Distracted and lonely, aloof from his crew, without anyone to confide in for years at a time, the famous and intimidating captain began to crack and lose his good judgment. Historians have proposed several different possibilities for Cook's erratic and volatile behaviour, including opium addiction, nerve pains, or vitamin-B deficiency caused by a roundworm infestation in his bowels (which would have produced symptoms such as depression, tiredness, lack of willpower, and irritability). Whatever the cause, it led directly to a disastrous and tragic series of events on February 14, 1779, in Kealakekua Bay in Hawaii.

Having spent nearly a month in the bay, the two ships left, only to return after a few days, when the *Resolution* was found to be in need of repairs again. The islanders' generous initial reception of the Europeans as nearly divine had by then shifted. They chafed at the obligation to feed and entertain several hundred guests and appeared disturbed when informed that the two ships were again to be anchored in the bay. After a series of thefts and some angry taunting, Cook awoke on the fourteenth to find the largest of the ships' boats missing. He flew into a rage and ordered cannons to blast any Native canoes in the bay. He then hastily organized a contingent of ten marines, sent two boats close to shore with armed sailors, and captured the Hawaiian king to ransom him for the return of the stolen boat. A mob of several thousand islanders awaited him on the beach, and Cook, sensing danger, released the hostage king and retreated to the shore with the marines.

As they retreated towards the boats, an islander drew a dagger and made a motion to throw a rock at Cook's back. Cook turned and fired his gun, then ordered his men to "take to the boats." The crowd rushed forward, the marines fired a volley, and in the ensuing melee Cook was stabbed and drowned in the surf. Four of the marines were also killed and many more were seriously injured, as were seventeen Hawaiians. Stunned and demoralized by their leader's death, the crew leapt into their small boats and fled back to the ships that were anchored in the bay. Meanwhile, the Hawaiians

James Cook began to crack under the strain of command during his third voyage of exploration. He was killed by a gang of angry Hawaiian Islanders in Kealakekua Bay on February 14, 1779. Portions of his dismembered body were later returned to his despondent crew.

mutilated Cook's body, hacking it to pieces and carrying it away into the forest. A few days later, a Hawaiian priest delivered to one of the ships a portion of a bloody thigh and a bag containing other body parts, including hands and a scalp, identified as Cook's. The English mariners, unrestrained by Cook's stern authority, went on a bloodthirsty, revenge-fuelled rampage, shooting islanders and burning their village. Dozens were killed before the *Resolution* and the *Adventure* finally departed.

A week later, Cook's dismembered body was ceremoniously pitched from the *Resolution* into the endless sea, a somehow fitting end for the man who, despite cracking under the strain of command, had spent the greater part of his life devoted to the health and well-being of his crew, pushing the limits of nautical technology and fundamentally altering the geographical understanding of the world. James Clerke, Cook's second-in-command, reluctantly assumed control of the ill-fated expedition, but without Cook to lead them the officers were not eager to continue the quest. After a half-hearted foray north the following spring, they headed for home. Clerke continued Cook's antiscorbutic regimen, and not a single mariner died from scurvy during the almost two years it took to reach England.

Although Cook had won the battle against scurvy, still no one knew exactly how. But the mystery had been taken from the dreaded scourge—it was indeed curable, and almost certainly by the inclusion of specific foods in a sailor's diet. But by the time Cook had departed on his third voyage in the summer of 1776, the window of opportunity for the testing and debate of antiscorbutics was quickly drawing to a close. With the War of American Independence, the Royal Navy was again called upon for strenuous action and was preoccupied with mustering thousands of new recruits. Haslar hospital was once again filled to capacity with sick, injured, and scorbutic mariners. When the news of Cook's death reached England, the nation was engaged in a pitched naval war.

Despite Cook's unparalleled success at preventing scurvy in the open sea, the navy failed to even try to understand why he had prevailed, and many more voyages left port with very uncertain futures. The onset of the war relegated scurvy research to the back burner. Ironically, just as the navy was called on to do its duty, the interest in combating scurvy ebbed and was supplanted by the complicated logistics of gearing up for war. Solving scurvy should have been a prime concern, yet somehow it was set aside as unimportant. Because the Admiralty was too preoccupied with the war to be concerned with continued trials, portable soup, sauerkraut, and wort of malt, which seemed to enjoy the greatest respect from both Cook and Pringle at the Royal Society, became the official antiscorbutics on board Royal Navy ships.

Nearly five years into the War of American Independence, in 1780, a thirty-one-year-old man destined to have a profound impact on global events was making his first voyage aboard a British man-of-war. He was an aristocratic physician, not a surgeon or a sailor. This man would pick up the dropped threads of scurvy's convoluted tapestry from where Lind and Cook had left off.

8

MAN OF INFLUENCE: GILBERT BLANE AND THE WEST INDIES FLEET

BY 1780 IT WAS OBVIOUS that the war was not going well for Britain and the Royal Navy. In the previous years, the nascent American states had secured as allies France (in 1778) and Spain (in 1779), and these countries sought to stunt British global expansion and preserve the balance of power in Europe by supporting the rebellion in Britain's colonies. The alliance effectively gave the American colonies a navy, and the war had taken a turn for the worse for Britain.

The Royal Navy had been forced to rapidly expand to meet the new challenges of a conflict that had evolved from a few thousand rebelling colonists to an international battle involving possible invasion from Continental Europe. The Royal Navy had increased in size from 103 ships of the line and 17,731 men in 1774 to 430 warships and 107,446 men by the end of the war in 1783. It was no small accomplishment to find and train about 90,000 sailors, construct the ships for them to sail, and reorganize and increase the victualling and supply for a navy that more than quadrupled in a handful of years. The quality and health of the sailors, many of them pressed into service, suffered, and the Admiralty devoted little effort to improving the provisioning and living conditions of the men.

The Channel fleet was the worst of all. The extent of scurvy and typhus there bordered on the disastrous by the final years of the war. Christopher Lloyd and Jack Coulter in their comprehensive work *Medicine and the Navy* detailed the sickly, debilitated state of the Channel fleet throughout the war, drawing especially on the reports of sea captains. In 1778 Captain Walsingham wrote, "The men I had from the former [ship] were composed of old men and boys, and instead of 50 I was to receive from the latter [ship], I could get but 25, the rest being sent round in a prize or devoured with scurvy, and those I did get were so affected with it that most of them have been on the sick list ever since they came on board." Captain Thompson wrote in 1778, "My ship is full of cripples and half recovered wretches from the hospital. I have not one seaman. Yet I am commanded immediately to the West Indies." Admiral Darby wrote to the lords of the Admiralty in 1781 that "scurvy is making strong strides, many ships have been but short time to port, so that if these ships are kept out long, they will be rendered useless for want of men."

In August 1779, the weakness of the Channel fleet nearly cost Britain her sovereignty. The Royal Navy was spread so thin that the Channel fleet was unable to defend against a combined French and Spanish fleet that appeared off the coast of Plymouth. But in this instance it was scurvy that *saved* Britain from invasion. The Spanish ships were delayed seven weeks before joining the French ships, and by the time they arrived in the Channel, scurvy had latched on to two-thirds of the French crews. The invasion fleet rushed back to port, losing the greatest opportunity France ever had of invading Britain. Lloyd and Coulter write that "it was said that so many dead were thrown overboard that the citizens of Plymouth dared not eat any fish for over a month."

On August 19, 1780, the Channel fleet returned from a short tour patrolling the choppy waters along the southern and eastern coasts of England and the Bay of Biscay with an unusually large number of sick mariners. Although never particularly far from land during this routine patrol, the fleet remained at sea for ten weeks, and twenty-four hundred sailors, fully one-seventh of the fleet, had come down with scurvy. Despite orders from the Admiralty to remain at sea, the fleet's commander, Admiral Geary, had no alternative but to put in to Haslar hospital for the relief of the sailors. "The great number of sick," wrote one observer, "especially scorbutics, made it indispensable." The sailors' condition was deteriorating quickly, and the fleet could not have remained at sea any longer without tremendous casualties.

It seems incredible that with the exception of the occasional ship governed by an enlightened captain and an informed surgeon, scurvy was raging through the navy to the same extent it had during the past century. Hadn't Cook already demonstrated in the course of nearly a decade at sea that scurvy could be held at bay indefinitely?

The continuing scurvy problem was explained in part by the fact that the hygiene and dietary practices aboard Cook's ships could not necessarily be duplicated on Royal Navy warships. Cook's voyage was a scientific and exploratory one, not a military one, and he had very different objectives. The nature of military planning was such that a warship couldn't go to shore whenever it needed antiscorbutic foods; it might be awaiting battle or engaged in a close blockade of a port, near to land but not able to replenish water or stores. But while the medical success of Cook's voyages was passed off as an accomplishment not reproducible by the navy, in reality the navy's problems had as much to do with the continuing use of ineffective antiscorbutic medicines as they did the uniquely unnatural sailing conditions imposed by a large fleet during times of war. The Admiralty believed that it was endorsing the strongest and most effective antiscorbutics available when it issued portable soup, sauerkraut, and wort of malt to all navy ships. And oddly, Cook himself, along with Sir John Pringle, was at least partly responsible for the Admiralty's continued use of ineffective medicines.

As we have seen, all the medical conclusions from Cook's antiscorbutic trials were based on a few ambiguous and conflicting statements he and his surgeons made following the first two voyages. From these strongly qualified statements, the Admiralty drew its official policy on antiscorbutics. Although Cook was basically unsure which of the foods he had used were the best, Pringle felt that Cook's records were certain proof that MacBride's wort of malt was the miracle antiscorbutic sought by the Admiralty.

While Pringle's great contribution to eighteenth-century medicine was to continuously advocate for improved cleanliness and ventilation in barracks and hospitals, his opinions on the cause and cure for scurvy were dubious, ill-founded, and perhaps self-serving. In hindsight, it appears that Pringle distorted Cook's records to favour wort of malt. During his speech to the Royal Society on the occasion of Cook's being awarded the Copley Gold Medal in 1776 (Cook himself was too busy to attend), Pringle selectively presented the material from Cook's journal to bolster his own favourable opinion of wort of malt and to downplay the reported benefits of citrus rob—a stance Cook never clearly took himself. "Before the power of the fixed air in subduing putrefaction was known," he said in his speech to the Society, "the efficacy of fruits, greens and fermented liquors was attributed to the acid in their composition." Despite a growing body of evidence that the theoretical foundations underpinning the use of MacBride's wort of malt as an antiscorbutic were flawed, Pringle continued to believe in its effectiveness. Other physicians reported that they had been unable to duplicate MacBride's experiment and halt the putrefaction of meat, while Lind claimed in the third edition of his treatise that he no longer believed scurvy to be a putrid disease, having never detected any putrefaction in the thousands of scurvy patients he regularly treated at Haslar.

Pringle, however, assumed that the concept of fixed air halting putrefaction was a given, and he concluded therefore that wort of malt was the most effective antiscorbutic because it freed the body's supply of fixed air. He then boldly claimed that Cook's surgeon found citrus rob to be "of so little advantage that, judging it not advisable to lose more time, he set about the cure with the wort only, whereof the efficacy he was certain." Coincidentally this fit nicely with his own and MacBride's publicized research on fermentation as a counteracting agent for putrefaction, and its acceptance would have saved him from the embarrassment of having his theories proved false after so many years. Perhaps Pringle clung too strongly to the ideas that seemed so promising in his youth and became blinded to the possibility that wort of malt was not a great scurvy cure. Perhaps he was embarrassed about his own support for a scientifically tenuous theory that he had once held so strongly, and sought to save face by whitewashing its defects. Or perhaps Pringle had an antipathy towards Lind and a stubbornness that prevented him from ever considering citrus rob.

Pringle's prejudice against the usefulness of citrus juice might have come from the rob's inconsistency, but it also had something to do with his friendship with Charles Bisset, the physician who in the 1750s had directly refuted Lind's claim that scurvy responded remarkably to fresh fruits and vegetables. Pringle might have been swayed by Bisset away from having an open mind about Lind's suggestions and towards a scurvy cure that meshed with his own early research. Years earlier, Pringle served as a medical consultant with the Duke of Cumberland at the Battle of Culloden, where the Jacobites were defeated in 1746. As a devout Hanoverian, Pringle likely shared with Bisset an antipathy to anyone he suspected of having supported the Jacobite cause, including Lind. Pringle also had a stubborn streak: in 1770 he watched while his young friend William Stark died from self-induced scurvy and refused to advise him to consume fresh vegetables or fruit juices. For whatever reason, Pringle endorsed wort of malt as the most effective antiscorbutic despite the conflicting reports of its value.

As president of the Royal Society, Pringle had influence. Furthermore, the Admiralty might have been selectively or wilfully blind for other policy reasons. After nearly fifteen years of antiscorbutic trials by John Byron, Samuel Wallis, and finally the famed Cook, the Admiralty was eager to have the matter settled. There was no interest in Lind's rob or other tedious and annoying hygienic measures because of the hassle and expense of implementing them. MacBride's wort of malt was a substance that appeared to be a miracle cure costing virtually nothing. Expense was definitely an issue. Before he departed on his third voyage, Cook himself appears to have been persuaded by Pringle that citrus rob would have little practical use because of its expense. "I entirely agree with you," he wrote to Pringle in response to an earlier letter, "that the dearness of the rob of lemons and oranges will hinder them from being furnished in large quantities, but I do not think this is so necessary for though they may assist other things, I have no great opinion of them alone."

With the selective presentation of Cook's medical reports, there appeared to be a consensus between the renowned master mariner, the man who had done more than anyone before to defeat scurvy, and the head of the pre-eminent scientific society of the nation. Certainly Cook did not boldly state that he was of the opinion that wort of malt was either useful or useless—he seems to have been almost deliberately vague, shying away from a definitive conclusion. Why would Cook, already unsure of the exact effect of any of the antiscorbutics used on his voyages, go against one of the leading men of science in the country? He had nothing to gain by doing so, and having no official medical or scientific training, he had no standing to refute Pringle's interpretation even if he had disagreed with it. It is entirely possible that Cook wrote vaguely of the beneficial powers of wort of malt because his patron and sponsor believed in it and he didn't want to offend such a forceful and opinionated man. Perhaps Cook felt it would have been impolitic and rude, or potentially career-damaging—it was already unusual for someone of his social standing to have risen so far. Definitely there was subtle pressure from the Admiralty itself for him to endorse wort of malt over other solutions (in his orders for his first voyage, Cook was specifically apprised in writing of the Admiralty's favourable opinion of wort of malt). Or perhaps Cook was merely being tactful and would have clarified his position had he not died in Hawaii. The historical record doesn't offer answers, and we will probably never know.

In any case, the apparent success of wort as an antiscorbutic distracted physicians and the Admiralty from closing in on an actual cure. When a merchant sea captain wrote the Admiralty a letter in 1786 informing them, out of a sense of duty, that he found that lemon juice mixed with French brandy always cured scurvy, the Sick and Hurt Board replied that "trials have been made of the efficacy of the acid of lemons in the prevention and cure of scurvy on board several different ships which made voyages round the globe at different times, the surgeons of which all agree in saying the rob of lemons and oranges were of no service, either in the prevention, or cure of that disease." All other things being equal, the great advantages that wort of malt held over other potential antiscorbutics was that it was cheap, easy to prepare, and could be stored indefinitely. The official prescription of wort of malt as an antiscorbutic, however, was worse than if the Admiralty had done nothing, for it gave false hope while wasting valuable time. The historian Sir James Watt has concluded that Cook's endorsement of wort of malt, however tentative, was "a disastrous error which condemned many thousands of seamen to death." If Pringle, out of professional pride or wilful blindness, further distorted Cook's record in support of wort of malt, thereby helping to formulate the Admiralty's policy on antiscorbutics, how many thousands of men died horribly from scurvy in the succeeding years because of it? And how might world events have gone differently if wort of malt had been sooner revealed a chimera?

When Admiral Sir George Rodney hoisted his flag and crossed the Atlantic to join the West Indies fleet in 1780, he could not have known it but he had with him in his retinue the man who would reform the navy's policy on antiscorbutics and ultimately save the nation from defeat decades later. The fashionable and well-connected Gilbert Blane had no naval experience and had never laboured belowdecks as a surgeon's mate or even as a surgeon. He travelled as the personal physician to the admiral, a position he had acquired through a mutual acquaintance the previous year. Blane hailed from a wealthy, respectable, and established Ayrshire family; he had studied arts and medicine at Edinburgh University, and had graduated from the Glasgow Medical School. It was unusual, probably unprecedented, when Rodney, in recognition of Blane's social standing and agreeable personality, elevated him to physician to the fleet before the ships had even crossed the Atlantic. It was a grand promotion for one so young and with no naval experience. It placed him above surgeons who had laboured for years on ships, surgeons of great experience who lacked Blane's social respectability and didn't have the ear of the admiral. The appointment was to have profound consequences.

Realizing perhaps that his lack of experience in naval medical matters did not bode well for his new appointment, Blane devoted time during the weeks-long voyage to reading several books and reports that would form the foundation of his approach to the health of mariners. Although his appointment was the result of "interest," Blane took his new responsibilities seriously. Always keen on impressing his superiors, he knew that his best chance lay in accomplishing something noteworthy while stationed overseas. Fortuitously, the medical books he chose to read with attentiveness were written by James Lind. He also pored over the medical documents and surgeons' reports from Cook's voyages. He later referred to both as invaluable insofar as the health of seamen were concerned. Blane may have read other tracts. Indeed, given the Admiralty's current promotion of wort of malt he certainly was exposed to MacBride's *Experimental Essays*, but he never made mention of it, good or bad.

A portrait of Blane from later in his life, the only portrait known to exist, shows a man confident and secure in his place in society. His clothes are simple, dark, and formal. A high, clear forehead is graced by a distinguished fringe of slightly unkempt hair that creeps down his jaw below sunken, intelligent eyes. His tight mouth curls with a hint of arrogance, and his strong countenance is rounded by high cheekbones, an aquiline nose, and a gently cleft chin. He is a man who appears comfortable with both his past and the prospects for his future: a man who has accomplished great things, is well aware of it, and accepts the accolades that are his due. Blane was called Chilblain behind his back because of his distant and chilly behaviour towards those he considered his social inferiors.

No doubt there was envy in the fleet as this young, inexperienced aristocrat assumed power over naval surgeons with years of service, telling them how to mind the health of their crews. Although Blane was a physician and a scholar with great administrative capacity, he was an irritating fellow to the dozens of other surgeons of lower status whom he dismissed as irrelevant and unimportant. He was firmly aware of his exalted place in the social hierarchy, disdainful of those beneath him, and sycophantic to those above him. Even in his scientific papers he name-drops, to let others know of his acquaintance with higher powers. Admiral Rodney is identified as "my friend and protector" and frequently stroked with comments referring to his "characteristic warmth of patriotism and loyalty."

Inserted into a medical dissertation are out-of-place references to his close association with other aristocrats. "When Sir Charles Douglas and I . . . saw the French Flag hauled down," he chimed, "stupefied as it were by an ecstasy of joy, we rushed into each other's arms and embraced." But with the unquestioned support of Admiral Rodney, Blane had to be obeyed. Fortunately, his advice was well grounded and based upon sound observation and research.

Blane began by taking stock of the situation. "I perceived," he wrote, "the most anxious and laudable pains taken to husband and preserve from decay all manner of stores, such as ropes, blocks, spars, gunpowder and arms. But however precious these may be as the indispensable weapons of war, it will not be disputed that human hands are equally so. Yet . . . it does not appear that this branch of duty has been studied with the like degree of anxiety as that which regards the inanimate materials of war." The health of the sailors of the fleet was in a shambles, and Blane instinctively knew not only that it could be improved but that it *must* be improved to realize the potential of the fleet and improve their odds in a conflict where they were outnumbered and without allies.

There were twenty-one warships and more than twelve thousand mariners stationed in the West Indies, which had become the major theatre for naval battles involving France, Spain, and England during the War of American Independence. The combined French and Spanish fleets were slightly larger than the British fleet, and the British fleet was also on duty helping the British army and blockading farther north, in the territory of the Thirteen Colonies. Although it was the Channel fleet that was the worst manned and suffered to an alarming and debilitating extent from scurvy and fever, Blane was appalled at the state of health of the British mariners in the West Indies.

His first act was to compile and distribute to all the ships' surgeons, at his own expense, a pamphlet on hygiene and diet based on Lind's and Cook's recommendations. He titled it *A Short Account of the Most Effectual Means of Preserving the Health of Seamen*, and in it he advised improving shipboard cleanliness, the regular washing of sailors' clothes and bedding, the removal of infectious sailors to hospitals, and, most important, the inclusion of citrus juice and wort of malt as daily dietary supplements. Blane neutrally observed that Cook preferred wort of malt while Lind preferred lemon and orange juice and rob, and he concluded that therefore both should be used, showing himself to be a man in tune with the realities of politics and influence.

To understand the problems he was dealing with, Blane began collecting statistics from throughout the fleet. He requested each ship's surgeon to report to him monthly on the state of the sailors' health, with a breakdown of "diseases, deaths, and other circumstances of ship's companies." For the first time, the Admiralty had an accurate picture of how disease was weakening naval power and how disease rates fluctuated with the seasons. Fevers rose during the hurricane season, while scurvy rates doubled in the late winter/early spring and dropped again by June, when fresh foods were more readily available. Blane reported that the death rate from disease in the fleet was an incredible one in seven when he arrived, with cases of scurvy outnumbering all other illnesses combined. Of 12,019 mariners, 1,518 perished from disease during his first year in the West Indies, and only 60 died from enemy action. It was a staggering loss of manpower that was caused, in Blane's opinion, by the men living for months at a time upon "sea victualling." He also reiterated an observation first made by Lind decades earlier. "There is at sea a dismal uniformity of life," he wrote, "favourable to indolence and sadness, and therefore tending to hasten the progress and aggravate the symptoms of the scurvy."

After ten months in the West Indies, Blane briefly returned to England with Admiral Rodney. The primary conclusion he drew was that "more can be done towards the preservation of the health and lives of seamen than is commonly imagined, and it is a matter not only of humanity and duty but of interest and policy." Although somewhat aloof and cool, Blane certainly valued the lives of the common sailors and strove in an administrative and medical capacity to improve their lot. He also pointed out the value that should be placed upon the life of a sailor, not just for humanitarian reasons but for tactical advantage. He suggested that the men should be managed as a limited resource, not as expendable flotsam from the lower classes. "Towards the forming of a seaman, a sort of education is necessary, consisting in an habitual practice in the exercise of his profession from an early period in life; so that if our stock of mariners should come to be exhausted or diminished, this would be a loss that could not be repaired by the most flourishing state of public finances; for money would avail nothing to the public defence without a sufficient number of able and healthy men, which are the real resources of a state, and the true sinews of war."

While in England, Blane busied himself preparing a brief memorial to the Admiralty outlining his reasons and arguments for improving the health of mariners. In it, he pointed out that "scurvy is one of the principal diseases with which seamen are afflicted, and this may be infallibly prevented, or cured, by vegetables and fruit, particularly oranges, lemons, or limes. . . . I am convinced that more men would be saved by such a purveyance of fruit and vegetables than could be raised by double the expense and trouble employed on the imprest service. . . . Every fifty oranges or lemons might be considered as a hand to the fleet, inasmuch as the health, and perhaps the life, of a man would be thereby saved." The Admiralty, however, refused Blane's request for an official supply of citrus rob, claiming that it had been proven ineffective by a surgeon on Cook's second voyage, and that it was in any case too expensive. Of wort of malt, one of the chief antiscorbutics that Blane was supplied with by the Admiralty, he wrote, "its powers were so inconsiderable that some of the surgeons denied that it had any." He quietly stopped using it.

Blane also strongly advocated for the improvement of naval hygiene as laid out in Lind's various books, dryly observing that "crowding, filth, and the mixture of diseases, are the great causes of mortality in hospitals." Because of his social standing, Blane was able to express his ideas in a forthright and clear fashion without fear of repercussions. "I beg leave again to call to mind," he admonished, "that 1,518 deaths from disease, besides 350 invalids, in 12,109 men, in the course of one year, is an alarming waste of British seamen, being a number that would man three of His Majesty's ships of the line." While his argument in favour of fresh foods and lemons and his recommendations for improved shipboard hygiene should have been persuasive, they had little impact on the lords of the Admiralty. Too distracted by the war effort to bother with diet, health, and hygiene, they made no official policy changes in response to Blane's memorials.

Despite the Admiralty's reluctance to consider his suggestions for the Royal Navy as a whole, Blane was nevertheless able to implement them throughout the West Indies fleet with Admiral Rodney's support and patronage. Rodney trusted and respected Blane as a colleague and social equal, rather than dismissing him as a socially inferior naval surgeon. Blane was confident enough to ask for Rodney's support and to articulate his request over dinner or port in the great cabin of the admiral's flagship, instead of sending him a note. Most naval surgeons would have been too timid to force the issue even if they understood the problem, and they would never have had the social opportunity to broach the subject in person. The great benefits of Blane's reforms were quickly evident, and Rodney remained firmly behind him throughout the final few years of the war.

By the end of the war in 1783, the death toll in the ships under his medical supervision had been reduced from one in seven men to one in twenty by his own calculations. Admiral Rodney later wrote of Blane's contribution to the improvement of the British fleet in the West Indies. "To Blane's knowledge and attention it was owing that the English Fleet was, notwithstanding excessive fatigue and constant service, in a condition always to attack and defeat the enemy." The robust state of health of the majority of the seamen in the West Indies fleet undoubtedly contributed to a major British victory against the French at the Battle of the Saints on April 12, 1782.

Near St. Lucia, Admiral Rodney's thirty-six ships of the line were in pursuit of "an equal force" of French in an attempt to engage them before they combined with a Spanish fleet of twelve more ships of the line for a planned invasion of Jamaica. The thirty-three French warships were commanded by François Joseph Paul de Grasse, who had led the French in a notable victory against the British the year before by providing the colonial army under Washington with naval support at Yorktown. Although the British had a three-ship superiority, the French had a greater broadside weight of iron shot by 4,393 pounds, owing to heavier guns on the lower decks ("broadside" is the term for the discharge of a full set of guns on one side of a warship). The two fleets hastily formed the line of battle and sailed past each other, the guns blazing away in terrific broadsides. Erratic winds and poorly executed sailing manoeuvres opened gaps in the French line, and Admiral Rodney ordered his flagship through the opening, with others following his lead wherever space permitted. It was an unusual and unprecedented manoeuvre. By passing through the French line, he was able to pound the French ships with both broadsides almost without counter-fire.

No doubt many factors contributed to the British victory, including their faster and more accurate gunnery, tighter discipline, and a little bit of luck, but Blane's analysis of the comparative health of the two fleets is revealing. Of 21,608 sailors and marines in the British West Indies fleet, only a few hundred were down with scurvy and only about a thousand with fever and around seven hundred with the flux (dysentery). Although the number of scorbutic sailors steadily increased in the weeks following the battle, Blane's anti-scorbutic measures, including the use of local limes, had had a great effect. "There was less sickness and less death from disease in this month [April] than any of the former twenty-three months. . . . Every ship, except two, might be said to be healthy, most of them were complete in men, well appointed with officers and well found in stores and provision. Conformable to this was the eagerness, the confidence, and resolution, which led them to success and victory." If Blane hadn't reduced the incidence of scurvy and other diseases in the fleet during the previous year, the number of sick would have made it impossible for the British ships to have sailed through the French line and opened up with both broadsides—they wouldn't have had the manpower to execute timely sailing manoeuvres and operate all the great guns.

The state of the British fleet was in stark contrast to that of the French fleet, the condition and health of which Blane studied after the battle. Many of the French ships were destroyed or seriously damaged by the British broadsides, with the decks covered in shards of exploded masts, downed sails, tangled rigging, and mutilated bodies. The death toll from the battle was staggering: on de Grasse's flagship, *Ville de Paris*, four hundred were killed and seven hundred wounded. Looking beyond the battle damage, Blane found the French ships in an appalling state of sanitation. "The discipline and internal economy of the French ships of war are greatly inferior to those of the British," he wrote. "Their decks are never washed and there is a great defect in every point of cleanliness and order. . . . There are not even scuppers opened on the lower decks as outlets to the water and filth. . . . The vent is a pipe, contrived on purpose, passing from that deck along the ship's side into the hold, which becomes thereby a common sink, inconceivably putrid and offensive. . . . The blood, the mangled limbs, and even whole bodies of men, were cast into the orlop, or hold, and lay there putrefying for some time. . . . When, therefore, the ballast, or other contents of the holds of these ships, came to be stirred, and the putrid effluvia thereby let loose, there was a visible increase in disease." Scurvy and fevers were rampant amongst the sailors, weakening the fighting power of the French ships (and infecting the British crews after the battle). Blane casually observed that "the sickness in the French fleet was still greater in the beginning of the war than in the British; and has been the case in all the wars of this century." The outcome of the battle would have been different if the British crews were in as poor condition as the French, or indeed if the French crews were in as good condition as the British.

The Battle of the Saints resulted in a staggering British victory that, although it had no influence on the outcome of the war with the American colonies, ensured that Britain kept her Caribbean colonies at the peace conference the following year. Blane's rejuvenation of his portion of the Royal Navy, the West Indies fleet, was one of the few naval victories in a miserable war with little to celebrate for the British. There is no doubt that the victory was a result of Blane's improvement of the overall health of the fleet in the months leading up to the battle.

That same year, Sir John Pringle died at the age of sixty-nine. He had resigned his position as the head of the Royal Society a few years earlier, in 1778. Only after Pringle's resignation and death was the road cleared for Blane to lobby successfully for more effective antiscorbutics. Social establishments need to be periodically cleansed of stagnant ideas, much in the way a forest is rejuvenated by fire. Without having to worry about ruffling important feathers or wounding stubborn pride, and without fear of damaging his own career by contradicting a man of great respect and standing, Blane could begin to shift policy in a new direction. With Pringle died the scientific establishment's support for wort of malt.

The end of the War of American Independence on September 3, 1783, likely caused the deaths of thousands more mariners than if the war had continued. With the end of the hostilities and the Treaty of Paris came the end of the need for a scurvy cure—before Blane could push for implementation of his reforms throughout the Royal Navy. The dire problem of scurvy abated after the war because the disease was no longer of vital importance. Although it undoubtedly cropped up in subsequent years, the fleets were not at sea for as long and could put into port for the relief of mariners without endangering military objectives or the security of the nation. Peace stalled interest in solving scurvy—with no impending crisis, scurvy could again be safely ignored, and only individual seamen paid the ultimate price. Blane left the Royal Navy for a lucrative private practice.

During the 1780s, Blane was appointed to St. Thomas's Hospital in London and became the personal physician to several well-known and wealthy members of the social elite, including the Prince of Wales and the Duke of Clarence. In 1786 he married, and eventually he had six sons and three daughters in his stately house on Sackville Street in London. During this time he also devoted himself to writing his famous book, *Observations on the Diseases Incident to Seamen*, which in many ways reiterates what Lind had written in the previous decades. Blane graciously credits him with the original ideas. "But of all the articles, either of medicine or diet, for the cure of the scurvy, lemons and oranges are of much the greatest efficacy," he writes in one passage. "They are the real specifics in that disease, if any thing deserves that name. This was first ascertained and set in a clear light by Dr. Lind."

Despite his somewhat grasping social aspirations, Blane was also a caring and intellectually modest man, striving for the betterment of the conditions of the common sailor long after he could have forgotten about them and retired to his comfortable medical practice. Blane also displayed a humility out of character for an eighteenth-century medical professional. Discussing the power of citrus juice

The British surrender to General George Washington at the Battle of Yorktown in 1781 effectively guaranteed the independence of the American colonies. If scurvy had not weakened the Royal Navy, the conflict might have ended differently.

against scurvy, he admitted that "upon what their superior efficacy depends, and in what manner they produce their effect, I am at a loss to determine, never having been able to satisfy my mind with any theory concerning the nature and cure of this disease, nor hardly indeed of any other." This sentiment of curiosity overriding pride, which would become all the more common in the nineteenth century, was the beginning of a more modern and clinical approach to medicine and science. This attitude placed the horse firmly before the cart, the facts before the conclusions—something that had been the reverse for centuries.

In 1793, France, four years into a bloody revolution against aristocratic rule, declared war against Britain. The beginning of the French Revolution revived the need for a scurvy cure, and in 1793 Blane advised his friend Sir Alan Gardener, a member of the Admiralty board, to load up on lemon juice for his voyage to the East Indies. On the voyage, the juice was regularly administered according to Blane's instructions; a mixture of two-thirds of an ounce of lemon juice with two ounces of sugar was poured daily into the sailors' grog. The seventy-four-gun warship *Suffolk* "was twenty-three weeks and one day on the passage, without having any communication with the land . . . without losing a man." Although scurvy had appeared, it was quickly brought under control by an increase in the lemon juice ration.

In 1795 Blane was appointed a commissioner to the Sick and Hurt Board. Using the results of the trial aboard the *Suffolk* and drawing on his own reputation, social standing, and intimate acquaintance with many of the lords of the Admiralty, he persuaded the Admiralty to issue lemon juice as a daily ration aboard all Royal Navy ships. He was successful on March 5, one year after Lind's death and forty-eight years after Lind had conducted his experiment aboard the *Salisbury* in the English Channel. The daily ration of lemon juice was increased slightly over the amount doled out on the *Suffolk*, to three-quarters of an ounce. "The power [lemon juice] possesses over this disease," Blane wrote, "is peculiar and exclusive, when compared to all the other alleged remedies." Blane's great achievement was to have the juice issued as a daily preventative—he understood the need to replace the body's ascorbic acid reserves as they were depleted, rather than waiting for the symptoms of scurvy to appear before attempting a "cure."

In defence of other naval surgeons and physicians, however, it should be noted that Blane was not the only one who appealed to the Admiralty about the need for more and better antiscorbutics, particularly lemon juice or rob. In the 1790s, many others, including Thomas Trotter, Frederick Thompson, William Northcote, and Leonard Gillespie, suggested similar solutions, but they were of too low social standing to have gained a personal audience with important members of the naval hierarchy, and so they resorted to letters, which were likely opened and read by a secretary who mailed a stock response. No doubt many naval surgeons and physicians were annoyed that Blane was given all the credit for an idea that was reasonably widespread but underappreciated.

Blane continued to serve on the Sick and Hurt Board until 1802, when he resigned and returned to private practice. During his tenure, he had also secured the supply of soap on ships and the supply of free drugs to naval surgeons (previously they were responsible for supplying their own drugs from their meagre pay, which often resulted in insufficient medical supplies on ships). In 1812 he was made a baronet, partly because of his role in reorganizing the medical department of the navy and advocating for the increased recognition of naval surgeons, and partly because of his influential contacts. No doubt he accepted the honour with equanimity, for he was well aware of the significant impact of his reforms on the prosperity and security of his nation. Throughout his life he continued to give lectures and to write, arguing for improved hygienic measures in the navy and the prevention of fevers, and he was in support of compulsory vaccinations to eradicate diseases such as smallpox. In 1829 he established a prize medal for medical officers in the Royal Navy. His wife died in a cholera epidemic in 1832, and he passed away two years later in London, on June 26, 1834, at the age of eighty-five.

Blane has since become known as the father of naval medical science, though in truth he was more of a social reformer than a scientist. Throughout his career, he remained focused on preventative, or social, medicine—not on the internal functions of the body and its organs or the specific causes of individual diseases, and certainly not on medical theory, but on the role a better-structured society could play in preventing many of the most common sicknesses by improving cleanliness, quarantine, vaccinations, diet, and living conditions. It is fitting that Blane's practical cure for scurvy in the Royal Navy lay as much in social policy as it did in medicine. Although military necessity was obviously a key motivating factor, also significant was the slowly dawning realization, at least by a handful of perceptive individuals, of the greater collective value to the nation of improving the overall condition of individuals, something Lind had argued for as early as the 1750s and Cook had implemented on a micro scale on his voyages.

A century and a half later, Surgeon Vice Admiral Sir Sheldon F. Dudley wrote in an essay in the republished second edition of Lind's treatise that "there is no need to be critical of Blane and condemn him as a snob. Thank God he was, if it meant that he had the power of using cajolery and flattery to get his own way with the powers that be. In those days everything was a question of patronage, and without Blane's popularity with Admiral Rodney and the rulers of the King's Navy, the country might have had to wait even more than forty years to see Lind's recommendations . . . put into force." Countless thousands of lives were saved within only a few years of 1795, as the Royal Navy was again mobilizing to tackle a new threat to national security—the rise of Napoleon in France.

BLOCKADE:
THE DEFEAT OF SCURVY
AND NAPOLEON

ON THE CLEAR, GUSTY MORNING of October 21, 1805, twenty-seven British ships of the line—massive floating castles with hundreds of mariners, red-coated marines, and as many as one hundred blackened iron twenty-four- and thirty-two-pounders protruding from the gun ports—closed on an equally impressive French and Spanish fleet of thirty-three warships that hastily assembled into a ragged battle line off Cape Trafalgar, near Cadiz on the south coast of Spain. Admiral Pierre Villeneuve commanded the combined French and Spanish fleet, while the celebrated Horatio Nelson commanded the British fleet. Nelson ordered his signals midshipman to raise on the halyard a final communication to the well-trained commanders of his ships. The anxious midshipman raised the series of coloured flags on the quarterdeck of the *Victory* and spelled out the message "England Expects That Every Man Will Do His Duty."

A good number of the British sailors, hardy tars who had known war with France for more than a decade, had seen battle before, and they knew what lay ahead—multi-layered oak hulls burst asunder by spiralling iron balls; ships' decks raked with grapeshot; great guns overheating and shattering, exploding near the gunners; bodies and limbs pulverized by shot and pierced by wooden shrapnel from splintering walls and masts; a horror of chaos and carnage, followed by the whimpering moans of the wounded. As the fleets drew near, the decks were sanded rough to prevent sailors from slipping in the anticipated slush of blood and gore, the bulkheads and walls of the officers' quarters were cleared for action, splinter netting was hung to prevent fighting men from being crushed by falling debris, and sharpshooters nestled into the rigging of each ship.

Nelson had divided his force into two squadrons. The *Victory* and the equally large first-rate *Royal Sovereign* led their warships towards Villeneuve's battle line at a ninety-degree angle in an attempt to break through and attack from both sides and isolate the French vanguard from the battle. It was a strategy that ran counter to the accepted and formalized rules of naval warfare (which held that the two lines should be parallel and sail past each other with guns ablaze), but it had proved brutally effective twenty-three years earlier at the Battle of the Saints and during Nelson's other celebrated engagements with the French at the Battle of the Nile and the Battle of Cape St. Vincent. Although the lead ships would have to withstand five or six broadsides before returning fire, when they did unleash their first broadside it would rake through the stern of the enemy ship. Nelson was counting on superior British gunnery and sailing expertise once they had broken the battle line.

The first broadsides were fired at the *Royal Sovereign* as she ploughed through the French battle formation. Firing a raking shot into the stern of the *Santa Anna* in return, the *Royal Sovereign* delivered a devastating blast that killed or wounded four hundred mariners and dismounted twenty great guns. Thirty men were wounded and fifty dead on the *Victory*, meanwhile, and terrible damage was inflicted to the prow of the ship before she too ploughed through

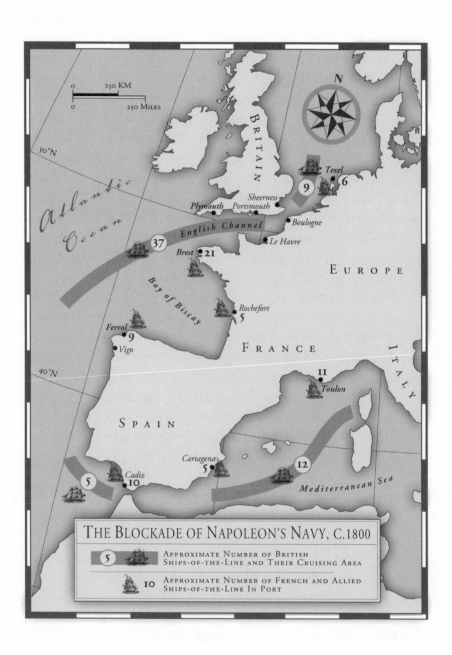

250 KM

250 MILES

N

50°N

Atlantic Ocean

BRITAIN

Texel

9

6

Sheerness
Plymouth Portsmouth

English Channel

Boulogne

Le Havre

37

Brest 21

EUROPE

Bay of Biscay

Rochefort

5

Ferrol

9

Vigo

FRANCE

I T A L Y

40°N

11

Toulon

SPAIN

Cartagena

5

12

Cadiz

5

10

Mediterranean Sea

THE BLOCKADE OF NAPOLEON'S NAVY, C.1800

5   APPROXIMATE NUMBER OF BRITISH
     SHIPS-OF-THE-LINE AND THEIR CRUISING AREA

10   APPROXIMATE NUMBER OF FRENCH AND ALLIED
     SHIPS-OF-THE-LINE IN PORT

the French line and fired her first broadside into the stern of the *Bucentaure.*

After the British ships shattered the French line, the battle degenerated into a furious melee between individual ships amidst clouds of acrid smoke, deafening cannon roar, and screaming men. Stripped to the waist in the sauna-like interior of the gun decks, with dirty bandanas wrapped around their heads to shield their ears, gunners raced to reload smoking hot cannons, cringing each time the blast shook the foundation of their wooden world and lobbed hundreds of pounds of iron shot in a fiery blast. Cutlass-swinging warriors flung themselves across the distance between ships, crawling through gun ports, scrambling over the gunwales, or clinging to dangling rigging and broken masts to engage the enemy hand to hand and take ships by force.

After nearly five hours of relentless battle, hulks of ships lay smashed, lurching aside with water flooding in through gaping holes. Masts and rigging were a tangled, crumpled mess; corpses were strewn about the blood-soaked decks. In the dark and swirling water, bodies bobbed between the wreckage and debris of the once majestic ships. One huge vessel burned uncontrollably, flames flickering in the evening sky and sending coiling plumes of oily black smoke upward. The moaning of dying and maimed men was a terrible dirge.

The events leading to this momentous battle had been set in motion months earlier by the diminutive Corsican general and tactical genius Napoleon Bonaparte. It was his attempt to end the stalemate at sea that had endured since England and revolutionary France went to war in 1793. Britain, in a shifting series of Continental alliances, had been at war constantly throughout this time (apart from a brief period of official peace between March 1802 and May 1803), and it would remain at war until Napoleon's defeat by a combined British and Continental army at the Battle of Waterloo in 1815.

Napoleon rose to prominence in the revolutionary government of France after brilliant military victories in the 1790s. He was a virtual dictator by 1799. He finally dispensed with the egalitarian ideals of the revolution altogether and crowned himself emperor in 1804. Ruthless and ambitious, he wanted nothing less than total European dominion, an accomplishment that remained elusive as long as Britain was free and supporting dissent through financial subsidies, with military supplies, and occasionally with troops. "Let us concentrate our efforts on building up our fleet and destroying England," Napoleon proclaimed in 1797. "Once that is done Europe is at our feet."

On land Napoleon was nearly invincible, but at sea British fleets controlled the trade routes and maintained a year-round watch on French ports. Although Napoleon had 130,000 troops in two thousand flat-bottomed invasion barges massed along the northern coast of France, he had been unable to transport them across the Channel because of the constant vigilance of and threat posed by the superior force of the Channel fleet. The Channel was only a few miles wide, and in good weather even unseaworthy barges could safely cross in a single day—assuming they had control of the Channel to protect them as they made the crossing. The French army was superior in numbers to British land forces, and vastly more experienced. Had troops landed in England, their victory would almost have been assured. The vast bulk of the French navy, however, and the ships of her Spanish allies were sheltered in ports ringing western Europe, from Texel in the English Channel to Toulon in the Mediterranean. The Continental blockade was intended not to prevent all ships from entering and leaving French and Spanish ports, or to destroy or harry Continental commerce (both Britain and France authorized thousands of independent privateers to prey on enemy commercial shipping), but to contain Napoleon's warships in port in small fleets and never to allow them to congregate into a single force without first having to contend with a British fleet of superior force. Although employed successfully in a limited capacity in the Seven Years' War half a century earlier, the blockade was a calculated gamble, and despite some early success in the late 1790s no one knew until 1805 whether it could repel an organized and concerted invasion effort.

The blockade had wearily dragged on for ten years before Trafalgar and would drag on for ten more. Fleets of ships of the line cruised for up to six months at a time back and forth along the same stretch of coast, through weather foul and fair, through spring, summer, and fall, and all through the winter gales, hoping to tempt a smaller force of enemy ships out into a battle to capture or destroy them. Fast-sailing frigates, cutters, and sloops prowled close to land, spying for evidence of a fleet leaving port, and rushed back to communicate with the ships of the line stationed farther out to sea. Transport ships occasionally brought new lemon juice supplies to the fleet. Through fortune of geography, Britain was in a position to dominate the seas of western Europe and block other European ships from crossing the Atlantic, and when storms lashed the coast, blowing blockading ships off station, the prevailing winds kept French and Spanish ships from leaving port.

This kind of operation was tiresome and tedious work for the tens of thousands of mariners crammed together on their ships with only their duty to keep them occupied. Although warships had grown in size throughout the century, so did the number of men needed to sail them. Anson's flagship, the *Centurion*, in the 1740s held sixty guns and about six hundred sailors, while at the Battle of Trafalgar sixty years later Nelson's flagship, *Victory*, had one hundred guns and more than nine hundred sailors. Larger, more heavily manned ships, combined with the need to remain at sea for months at a time, multiplied the critical responsibility for effective provisioning. At one time, ships were refitted and reprovisioned

The diminutive Corsican general Napoleon Bonaparte (1769–1821) was a military genius who seized power in France in the late 1790s. He finally dispensed with the egalitarian ideals of the French Revolution altogether and crowned himself emperor in 1804.

in the winter following the summer battle season, as was the case when Blane first sailed to the West Indies in 1780. During the wars with revolutionary and Napoleonic France, however, ships were in action year-round to keep up the blockade.

The blockade had thwarted several small-scale invasion attempts before 1805. In December 1796, more than thirteen thousand French troops and seventeen ships of the line cruised off Bantry Bay in Ireland but did not land. They were waiting for the Irish revolutionaries to revolt and feared retaliation from the larger Channel fleet. In 1798, after the Irish rebellion, twelve hundred French troops did land at Bantry Bay, but they were taken and reinforcements by sea were blocked by the Royal Navy. In 1797, a small French force came ashore in Wales but was also hastily defeated. In October 1797, Napoleon ordered the construction of the flat-bottomed invasion barges to transport his troops across the Channel. The threat of invasion was real and direct and tangible, and the long-suffering mariners of the Royal Navy were called upon as never before to defend their homeland.

By 1805, Napoleon's invasion army had been camped in northern France for nearly two years, and in March of that year, he issued orders to combine the disparate components of his navy into a mighty battle fleet that would then provide safe passage for his troops across the English Channel. He ordered Admiral Villeneuve in Toulon to evade the blockading Mediterranean fleet, sail west to Cadiz, drive away the smaller British squadron, liberate the Spanish ships, and quickly flee across the Atlantic to Martinique. Admiral Honoré-Joseph Ganteaume was to sally forth from Brest, escaping the Channel fleet, and proceed south to the northern Spanish port of Ferrol, liberate the fleet contained there, and head to the rendezvous in Martinique. And Admiral Edouard Thomas Missiessy was to lead the French fleet from Rochefort directly to the rendezvous. If all went according to plan, Napoleon's grand fleet would comprise about eighty ships of the line and more than twelve frigates. By crossing the Atlantic first, Napoleon hoped to cause some damage to British shipping in the West Indies, but most important he hoped to confuse the British fleets and conceal his true intentions. The grand fleet was then to recross the Atlantic and cruise up the English Channel in sufficient force to crush the Channel fleet and secure the strait for his troops. It was a strategically sound plan that would have worked had it not proved impossible for many of his ships to escape the British blockade.

Ganteaume's twenty-one ships of the line were met by a superior British force each time they manoeuvred out of Brest and so were unable to free the nine warships in Ferrol and proceed to Martinique. Although Missiessy succeeded in crossing to Martinique with his five warships, he grew tired of waiting for the other squadrons and returned to Rochefort when they failed to rendezvous in May. Villeneuve and his warships successfully eluded the Mediterranean fleet, freed the Spanish warships at Cadiz, and crossed to Martinique, but they arrived after Missiessy had returned to Rochefort. Villeneuve then received new orders to prey on British shipping in the West Indies for a month before sailing to relieve the ships at Ferrol and then Brest, and continuing with the invasion plan. In June, however, he learned that Nelson and the Mediterranean fleet had followed him west across the Atlantic, after first searching for him near Egypt, and so he departed immediately, hoping to elude them again. Villeneuve's month-long voyage back to Europe was disastrous, with storms, scurvy, and fevers killing a thousand of his sailors and weakening thousands of others. On July 22, in thick fog near Ferrol, he encountered a small British fleet of fifteen warships under Sir Robert Calder. Disoriented, with damaged ships and weakened men, Villeneuve fought to escape after losing two ships and then retreated to the nearby port of Vigo, where he recuperated and repaired his damaged fleet. Villeneuve knew that pressing on with the original plan would be hopeless, as the entire British fleet now knew of the invasion scheme and would be lying in wait at the entrance to the Channel. He decided to cruise south to Cadiz, arriving on August 22—four and a half months after leaving Toulon, most of which had been spent at sea.

On September 28, Napoleon ordered Villeneuve to return with his fleet of thirty-three warships to the Mediterranean to help transport troops to Naples. Nelson and a twenty-seven-warship battle squadron waited offshore, and they clashed on October 21, off Cape Trafalgar. By that evening, nineteen of the French and Spanish ships had been destroyed or struck their colours and surrendered. Others burned, and in the coming days several more were taken or destroyed. The remainder of the combined fleet limped back to Cadiz, leaving the British victorious. But the victory was tempered by loss. At four-thirty in the afternoon, the great commander Nelson, the man who had led British fleets on their greatest string of victories in history, was blasted through the chest by a sniper. He later expired in the gloomy sweat- and blood-soaked cockpit deep in the bowels of his battered flagship. "Thank God I have done my duty," he reputedly gasped with one of his final breaths.

Trafalgar would be Nelson's greatest victory. The death toll was tremendous: 448 British seamen were killed and 1,241 wounded, while 4,408 French and Spanish were killed and 2,545 wounded. Another 14,000 French and Spanish were taken prisoner. A day after the terrible engagement, the wind picked up and pulled whitecaps from the turbulent sea. A great storm was brewing—a natural counterpart to the bloody massacre. Dark clouds rolled in from open water, wind shrieked in the rigging, and the sea surged, sucking the ships towards a rocky lee shore. Many of the ships were already badly damaged, with masts cracked, rigging tangled together, sails shredded, and water flooding through holes in the hull—not the best conditions for riding out a storm. And with the great number of casualties and prisoners, many of the ships could not be fully manned. For days the storm raged, and eventually the British officers ordered the tow cables to several of the French and Spanish prizes cut. They were turned loose into the storm, some with wounded mariners still struggling to survive in the dank holds. Only a handful of Napoleon's ships escaped the disaster of war and natural calamity. At Trafalgar the British tore the heart out of Napoleon's navy, and the defeat of scurvy had played a significant role in their supreme victory.

Many of the naval commanders who led the Royal Navy to victory at Trafalgar were old enough to remember a time when scurvy was as great a foe, and perhaps more feared, than the enemy. Nelson himself nearly perished from the disease in 1780, when he was twenty-two years old and had been promoted despite his youth to captain of the twenty-eight-gun British frigate *Albemarle* during the War of American Independence. The ship had been eight weeks at sea, voyaging to Quebec for convoy duty. As the disease took hold, the young captain and his men became weakened and melancholy. Dark splotches appeared on their skin, and their gums began to swell painfully. The only food they had was salted sea rations, and they were in danger of perishing, leaving the ship a drifting bonebed. Before anyone had succumbed to the dreadful affliction, however, they were miraculously delivered from their predicament by the appearance of a small American vessel from Plymouth, Massachusetts. The American captain, perhaps pitying their miserable condition, graciously shared with them some live chickens and fresh vegetables. The men soon recovered, and the *Albemarle* continued on its voyage to the St. Lawrence. Fortunately, the foods and climate of Quebec, very near to where Jacques Cartier and his crew suffered from scurvy two and a half centuries earlier, was sufficient to recruit the young captain's constitution. "Health," Nelson wrote to his father, "that greatest of blessings, is what I never truly enjoyed till I saw fair Canada."

The Battle of Trafalgar on October 21, 1805. The British tore the heart out of Napoleon's navy and thwarted the invasion of England. The defeat of scurvy played a significant role in their supreme victory.

When Nelson died at Trafalgar, he was at the pinnacle of a brilliant naval career. He was Britain's greatest commander, a national hero associated more closely than any other with naval supremacy during the Age of Sail. During the era of his stunning victories, in the late 1790s and early 1800s, scurvy was no longer a threat to the Royal Navy. It had been reduced to a menacing phantom, rarely occurring since Blane had persuaded the Admiralty to issue a daily dose of lemon juice as a preventative in 1795. Yet Nelson might easily have perished, like many others, before ever realizing his potential. Perhaps remembering his own encounter with scurvy as a young captain, he was devoted to the health of his men, which he knew contributed to the strength of his fighting force. He purchased additional supplies of lemon juice, above the Admiralty's regular issue. In February 1805, just a month before he set off on the pursuit of Villeneuve that culminated in the Battle of Trafalgar, he ordered for the Mediterranean fleet an astonishing twenty thousand gallons of lemon juice to supplement the regular issue of thirty thousand gallons. Despite having been months at sea without any significant time in port, the British sailors at Trafalgar were free from scurvy.

Although the Battle of Trafalgar was a stunning victory for Britain, the blockade strategy had already come to fruition a month earlier, on August 27, when Napoleon, realizing the total failure of his plan to combine the disparate fleets of his navy, ordered his invasion army in northern France to decamp to Austria, leaving Britain in command of the sea and free from the imminent threat of invasion. The blockade was a devastating strategy that kept Napoleon out of England and led ultimately to his defeat ten years later. "Those far distant, storm-beaten ships upon which the Grand Army never looked," wrote the naval historian Admiral Alfred Thayer Mahan, "stood between it and the dominion of the world."

Napoleon had thought it would be impossible for the British to maintain a year-round blockade. It was a terrible strain on Britain's naval resources and shipyards. It was also a terrible strain on Britain's seamen, and would have proved an unbearable strain had scurvy not been virtually eliminated from Royal Navy ships. Only the blockade stood as a bulwark against Napoleon's armies, and the fleet could not have done its job if the warships were continually scuttling back to port to discharge thousands of scorbutic sailors into hospitals and wait for them to regain their health before setting out again.

A single crippling incident such as what Lind dealt with in August 1780, when twenty-four hundred scorbutic mariners were landed at naval hospitals despite orders to keep at sea, could have broken the defence of the island and given Napoleon the opportunity to launch his invasion. But with the defeat of scurvy, the warships of the Royal Navy never deserted their posts and the majority of Napoleon's navy was kept bottled up in half a dozen separate ports throughout the war. The blockade disrupted France's commerce and communication with her colonies, damaged the French economy, and weakened the country's capacity to pay for the ongoing war. The British economy, on the other hand, although fluctuating throughout the war, grew stronger as its exports and imports flourished with the beginning of the Industrial Revolution. Having the run of the seas, the Royal Navy protected Britain's colonial interests while starving and isolating those of her enemies.

By the early nineteenth century the Royal Navy was consuming fifty thousand gallons of lemon juice annually, most of that coming through the naval base at Malta, one of the few Mediterranean ports not blocked by the French or the Spanish. Between 1795 and 1814, more than 1.6 million gallons of lemon juice were issued to Royal Navy ships. The juice was stored in bung-tight casks under a layer of olive oil, which although not a perfect preservative over a long time period retained enough ascorbic acid to fend off the advances of scurvy. Fresh lemons were salted, wrapped in paper, and stored in light crates or pickled in sea water or olive oil, their

Horatio Nelson (1758–1805) was Britain's greatest naval commander, a national hero more closely associated than any other with naval supremacy during the Age of Sail. During the era of his stunning victories in the late eighteenth and early nineteenth century, scurvy was no longer a threat to the Royal Navy.

juice squeezed shipboard by the cook or the surgeon's mate to be added to the grog. For the first few years after 1795, lemon juice was merely issued on demand to ships and fleets. In 1799, however, daily lemon juice became official issue to all ships of the Royal Navy because of the persuasions of Thomas Trotter, the physician of the Channel fleet, and Gilbert Blane's continued agitations. It was expensive, but the benefits far outweighed the cost.

The transformation of the health of British seamen following the introduction of lemon juice was immediate and remarkable. During the nine years of the War of American Independence, for example, the average annual ratio of sick and hospitalized mariners was about one in four, but in the nine years following 1795 the figure had been reduced significantly, to roughly one in eight. The naval historians Christopher Lloyd and Jack Coulter have made an interesting comparison of the incidence of fevers and scurvy at Haslar hospital. In 1782, scurvy afflicted 329 men per thousand while fever affected 112 men per thousand. In 1799, however, the proportion of men hospitalized with scurvy had fallen to 20 per thousand while fever had increased slightly to 200 per thousand (although fever was also on the decline by the early nineteenth century, owing to improved shipboard hygiene). Before the turn of the nineteenth century, scurvy accounted for less than 2 percent of mariners in the Royal Naval hospitals.

"Other causes," Blane wrote decades afterwards, "particularly the improved methods by which fevers were diminished, contributed greatly to this decrease of sickness, so that it may be difficult to assign precisely what is due to lemon juice. But what admits of no ambiguity, is that, ever since the year 1796, scurvy has almost disappeared from ships of war, and naval hospitals." By the early nineteenth century, most of the Admiralty sick lists did not even include scurvy as one of the common and standard sea diseases. Dr. John Lind, the son who took over Haslar hospital when James Lind resigned, informed Blane in 1815 that he had seen only two cases of scurvy in the final four years of the war. Trotter wrote in 1802 that during his early days in the Royal Navy, "it was no uncommon thing in those times for a ship during an eight week cruise to bury 10 to 12 men in scurvy, and land fifty at a hospital." But he noted that now when scurvy appeared, it was quickly treated.

The state of the fleet during the Nelsonian era of British naval supremacy was poles apart from its condition a mere two decades earlier, when Lind presided over the hospitalization of thousands of mariners of the Channel fleet in 1780. The Channel fleet, wrote Blane, "was overrun with scurvy and fever, and unable to keep the sea, after a cruise of ten weeks only; and let the state of this fleet be again contrasted with that of the Channel Fleet in 1800, which, by being duly supplied with lemon juice, kept the sea for four months without fresh provisions, and without being affected with scurvy." Blane observed with great understatement that "the year 1796 may therefore be considered as an era in the history of the health of the navy."

In the preface to an 1853 reprint of the narrative of George Anson's voyage, the editor, after discussing the horror of that particular bout with scurvy, wrote that "the reader will be satisfied to learn, that the fatal disease which reduced Anson's squadron to extremity, and has caused the loss of tens of thousands of our seamen, is now scarcely known either in public or private ships belonging to Great Britain. A due regard to cleanliness, warmth, and ventilation, but, above all, the free use of lime juice, or other acids, with fresh meat and vegetables as often as they can be procured, have almost, if not quite, annihilated the scurvy, which now but rarely appears, except under circumstances where these precautions are neglected, and may be said to exist only in the painful memory of those who have witnessed its fatal devastation."

Although it is difficult to quantify the specific impact of the defeat of scurvy on the outcome of many of the key naval battles and engagements of the French Revolution and the Napoleonic Wars, there can be no doubt that it played a significant role. In addition to enabling the blockade, it ensured that experienced British seamen didn't perish at an unsustainable rate during the years of the blockade. Blane calculated that if the severe mortality rate of British sailors during the War of American Independence had continued during the twenty-two-year conflict with France, the Royal Navy would have run out of sailors. "The whole stock of seamen would have been exhausted," he wrote, "in which case men would not have been procurable by any bounties however exorbitant; for it has been stated, that if the mortality of 1813 had been equal to that of 1779, there would have died annually six thousand, six hundred and seventy-four men more than have actually died: which in twenty years would have amounted to 135,480, a number very nearly equal to the whole number of seamen and marines employed in the last years of the war." If scurvy had continued to cull British seamen at its usual rate, the manpower of the Royal Navy would have been insufficient to meet the challenge of the prolonged war with France and the stresses of blockade duty. Britain had a population of only about nine million at the time, while France had more than twenty-five million. Writing after the Napoleonic Wars, the naval surgeon Robert Finlayson commented, "It is the opinion of some of the most experienced officers that the blockading system of warfare which annihilated the naval powers of France could never have been carried on unless sea-scurvy had been subdued."

The victory over the most malignant and destructive of maritime diseases was so complete that within a few years of Blane's recommendations being implemented, scurvy had lost its deadly and sorrowful connotations in the Royal Navy. It still cropped up occasionally on ships that were unable to obtain lemon juice or whose supply ran low on long voyages, but it was no longer the universally dreaded killer it once had been. Scurvy had been defeated.

Throughout the battles of the French Revolution and the Napoleonic Wars, the ships of the Royal Navy routinely defeated the French. Not only were the British sailors mostly disease-free but the crews were better trained and more experienced, owing to their extensive time at sea. France had a shortage of experienced officers because many were of aristocratic lineage and so were killed or exiled during the revolution. The surviving officers and crews gained little sea experience while locked up in port by British blockades, so when they did emerge and engage British ships, they were outmanoeuvred and outgunned. The Royal Navy had better officers and stricter discipline, and the crews were highly motivated, partly by the prospect of prize money from captured ships. The French needed great numerical superiority to have even a fighting chance against the precision machines of the Royal Navy. At Trafalgar, for example, the Spanish ships contained a large number of recently pressed men from the slums of Cadiz, many of the gunners had never practised firing from a ship rolling at sea, and a typhus epidemic raged throughout the fleet. The Spanish captains also resented being under the command of a French admiral. It is not surprising that they lost the battle, Nelson's innovative tactics aside.

Blane wisely pointed out that "it must however appear clear to every reflecting mind, that the care of the sick and wounded is a matter equally of policy, humanity and economy. Independently of men being sentient beings and fellow creatures, they may also be considered as indispensable mechanical instruments." If the "mechanical instruments" that powered and controlled the ships and guns were faulty, in disrepair, and generally in poor and unreliable condition, then the overall fighting force would also fail to achieve its potential. It doesn't take great imagination to picture the outcome of a battle between two ships of the line of equal size and armament, one with a vigorous, strong, and motivated crew, the other with a third of the mariners weakened, debilitated, and morose with scurvy.

There is evidence that the French and the Spanish knew of the antiscorbutic powers of citrus fruit but lacked the political will to implement the cure on an institutional level. A Spanish naval physician, Don Antonio Corbella, for example, wrote of his experience with scurvy in the hospital in Montevideo in 1794. A ship had crossed from Cadiz with "all its crew and staff infected with scurvy" to such an extent that "when they fell on the floor they could not get up and to many it was necessary for the nurses to feed them." Although Corbella prescribed a laxative "to clean the stomach and the first part of the large intestine from putrid material which are formed there," he also made "abundant use of lemonade" and "pure lemon juice . . . according to the strength of each one." The ship's surgeon had lacked the resources to cure the sailors during the voyage, and it was only when they reached port and the hospital that Corbella "was able to destroy this terrible disease and to free those unfortunate fellows who could now continue their voyage." Unable to benefit from the fundamental institutional restructuring that had eliminated scurvy in the Royal Navy, the French and Spanish crews continued to be ravaged by the disease on long voyages.

Without the political will to change centuries-old traditions in victualling and the education of surgeons, no large-scale cure of scurvy would have been possible for any nation. Napoleon was a brilliant strategist, but his focus was always on land and his interest in the navy was primarily as a means to move his troops and to tie up Britain's resources. If he had turned his strategic mind to reforming his navy, as he had reformed the organizational structure of his armies, the French and Spanish fleets would almost certainly have fared better in many of the numerous smaller-squadron or single-ship actions of the war. An invasion of Britain, however, would still have been dependent on breaking the Continental blockade and seizing naval control of the Channel, which would have been impossible without the failure of the Royal Navy.

Because of the blockade, a majority of French and Spanish ships spent most of their time in or close to port, seldom setting off on long voyages and so seldom suffering from scurvy. When they did venture forth on extended trips, such as during Pierre Villeneuve's evasive cruise across the Atlantic and back in 1805, scurvy and other diseases eventually caught up with them. Napoleon never initiated a naval blockade of British shipping or ports, so the discovery of a cure for scurvy would have had little tangible impact on his naval strategy. The historian Richard Harding writes in *Seapower and Naval Warfare, 1650–1830* that "the practical problems of engaging in a trade blockade based upon squadrons of large warships were too great to be considered a reasonable employment of the state's resources. Britain was probably alone in that a trade blockade converged with policies that were essential for its own survival— defence of its own trade and territorial integrity—and thus possessed the political will to develop the resources that made such a blockade possible." The ball was in Britain's court. The terrible outcome from not discovering a cure for scurvy on Royal Navy ships— an inability to effectively maintain the two-decade blockade of enemy ports—would have been borne by the British alone, just as the cure for scurvy provided them with the greatest benefit, their very survival as a nation.

What if Britain had discovered scurvy's cure a decade and a half earlier, just after Cook's return from his second voyage, when the evidence in favour of citrus juice and against wort of malt should have been compelling? Blane observed that by the early nineteenth century, it was commonly accepted within the navy that because of the reduced death toll and the improved health and strength of mariners after 1795, two ships of war were more powerful than three in "former times." "When the Fleet could not keep the sea for more than ten weeks without being unserviceable by scurvy," Blane wrote, "another force as nearly equal as possible had to be available to replace it." The former times that Blane referred to included the War of American Independence, during which, as we have seen, the Channel fleet in particular was in a shambles because of scurvy. A mere ten years separated that war and the Napoleonic Wars. The naval historians Christopher Lloyd and Jack Coulter have concluded that "the state of the navy from a medical point of view was so bad between the years 1778 (when the war became general) and 1783 that it must be accounted partly responsible for the defeat which Britain suffered."

What might have been the outcome of the War of American Independence had lemon juice been the official antiscorbutic at that time instead of the ineffective wort of malt? With the Royal Navy unhindered by scurvy, and the ships a third stronger in terms of manpower, would the entry into the war of France and Spain on the side of the American colonies have been great enough to secure their independence from Britain? The practical example of the Royal Navy's blockade potency against Napoleon is compelling. The historian Paul Kennedy has noted in *The Rise and Fall of British Naval Mastery* that the British decision not to implement a blockade of France in 1778, which would have been virtually impossible without first solving the problem of scurvy, allowed "free egress for all the French squadrons which were dispatched to assist Washington, to intervene in the West Indies. . . . The saving of wear-and-tear on British warships simply transferred the problem of establishing naval control to more distant seas." If the Royal Navy had been able to maintain a naval blockade of France and Spain as effective as the blockade that proved so devastating during the French Revolution and the Napoleonic Wars, a large French fleet would not have been able to freely cruise the Caribbean and sail to the aid of Washington's army on the shores of Chesapeake Bay in 1781. Without the pressure wrought by several thousand French troops and twenty-eight ships of the line, General Charles Cornwallis probably would not have surrendered at Yorktown on October 22 and effectively guaranteed the independence of the American colonies. Kennedy notes that "the interventions of the French navy, in the Channel, off Gibraltar, in the West Indies, off Yorktown, had clearly played a considerable part in Britain's failure to win the war in America."

It can be argued that just as Britain owes its success against Napoleon and the dominance of the seas to the sagacity and perseverance of Gilbert Blane in 1795, the Thirteen Colonies and their allies in the War of American Independence owe their success against Britain to the overweening, stubborn pride, or wilful blindness, of Sir John Pringle, who influenced the Admiralty in favour of an antiscorbutic regimen that had little effect in reducing scurvy, which in turn severely weakened the strength of the Royal Navy.

Historians have pointed out that it is unlikely that the British could have held on to America indefinitely, regardless of their determination and strategy. Kennedy, for example, notes wryly that "by 1778 there were over 50,000 troops in North America and they were showing singularly little sign of achieving victory. . . . Even if the main rebel forces had been annihilated, there remained the difficulty of preserving this dominance over a resentful, populous and resourceful American people under such arduous geographical and logistical circumstances." The war in America was an organizational nightmare for the British, with all the supplies for both the army and the navy coming, at unpredictable intervals, across the vastness of the Atlantic Ocean. As well, the British fleet had been allowed to deteriorate after the Seven Years' War, and in the American Revolution, unlike previous wars, Britain fought without Continental allies to occupy France and Spain. The Americans were fighting for their homeland, and the determination of the colonists to shake off Britain's yoke would have made it nearly impossible to subdue them indefinitely.

But with an effective British blockade of American, French, and Spanish ports, the American colonies would have had their victory delayed for years and would have agreed to different terms at the eventual peace conference. At no other point in history did scurvy have the ability to affect world events to such an extent. In times of peace, the secret of scurvy's cure would have spread quickly between navies and merchants, simply because sailors always changed ships and talked with others in their profession. But during the cauldron of war in Europe in the late eighteenth century, the timing of Britain's discovery and implementation of a cure for scurvy on an institutional level in the national navy changed the course of world history.

In terms of its larger impact on world affairs, Blane's daily ration of lemon juice for mariners was perhaps the single greatest medical and socio-military advancement of the era. After the defeat of Napoleon, Britain's position as the leading European, if not world, power was assured—with this terrible bloodbath, the country was propelled to the pinnacle of political and commercial dominance, the only superpower of the era and the maintainer of "the peace of Britain." The Royal Navy emerged as the strongest fleet on the globe, but, free from scurvy, the seas were opened to commerce, travel, and exploration for many nations. Knowledge of the practical cure for scurvy would have spread quickly once regular commerce and travel resumed in Europe—and it was a crucial development for world prosperity. With a lower death toll of mariners on long voyages, the expense of manning ships and shipping goods was greatly reduced. Without scurvy tethering ships to port, global trade expanded throughout the nineteenth century, fuelling the Industrial Revolution. Medical reasoning began a slow departure from the theoretical foundations that had stultified practical inquiry for centuries. And tens of thousands of lives all over the world were saved. The defeat of scurvy, and the concomitant increase in the time ships could spend at sea, was the keystone in the construction of the British-dominated global trade and communication network that flourished throughout the nineteenth century.

Many of the other technological improvements of the Nelsonian era, such as standardized signalling, copper sheathing on the hulls of ships, and the calculation of longitude through the use of an accurate naval chronometer, would have been of little practical use if the health of seamen had not also been correspondingly improved. "Without the supply of lemon juice," Blane wrote, these advances which "do honour to the human intellect, particularly to the age and country in which we live, would be in a great measure frustrated." What good was the ability to accurately calculate longitude and thereby remain at sea indefinitely if the mariners perished from scurvy because of it? What good would have been bigger merchant ships for transporting greater quantities of goods on longer voyages between ports if the sailors' health was insufficient for the task?

The conquest of scurvy was certainly not the only factor in Britain's defeat of Napoleonic France or her subsequent commercial expansion and rise in global power. Historians have studied and written in great detail about the complicated blend of factors, including geography, natural resources, taxation policies, government, and economics, that resulted in Britain's preeminence in the nineteenth century. But the conquest of scurvy is an underappreciated foundation upon which these other achievements were built. It has been observed by the historian S. R. Dickman that "one might say the British Empire blossomed from the seeds of citrus fruits." And given that the empire was maintained in great part by the effectiveness of its fleet, it is hard to disagree. The conquest of scurvy as a widespread occupational disease in the Royal Navy, and later for all the world's mariners, was a crucial link in the chain of events that has led to the world as we know it.

EPILOGUE:
THE MYSTERY SOLVED

NEITHER JAMES LIND nor James Cook lived to see the tremendous benefits to the Royal Navy brought about by the defeat of scurvy. While he effectively eliminated scurvy aboard his ships, Cook left a vague and muddled report on antiscorbutics that was later used by John Pringle to promote a fashionable but useless cure that contributed to the Royal Navy's problems during the War of American Independence. Still, Cook is often erroneously given credit for the defeat of scurvy, and opinions of Lind have not been consistently favourable. During Lind's own life, he remained an obscure and perhaps not entirely respected individual—he received no national honours and was never elected a fellow of the Royal Society. He was ignored and forgotten by almost everyone, apart from a few perceptive disciples. By the mid-twentieth century, however, he was regarded as the founder of naval hygiene, with some writers claiming that he alone solved the scurvy problem, and that he understood why citrus fruits were powerful medicines against scurvy, which clearly he did not. Now a more balanced appreciation of his character and accomplishments highlights both his successes and his failures, which should not minimize his over-all contribution to solving the mystery of scurvy. The climate of theories and ideas in which he laboured was so convoluted that to overcome it required more energy than one single man could have mustered, and it is a testament to his integrity and strength of character that he persevered in promoting what were obviously unpopular ideas that ran counter to prevailing notions. Without Lind's work as a foundation, and Cook's morale-boosting success against scurvy in the Pacific, Blane would have had little informa-tion upon which to base his own efforts to eradicate the affliction.

More than half a century after Blane helped eliminate scurvy from the Royal Navy, and several decades after his death, the disease resurfaced in Europe. It was still not entirely understood. In the mid-nineteenth century, limes from British plantations in the West Indies had been substituted for Mediterranean lemons because they were a source of citrus juice securely under British control. Merchant sailors of the East India Company, who frequently crossed the Atlantic on their return voyages pushed by winds and the Gulf Stream, became known as "lime juicers" because of the great quantity of limes they purchased in the West Indies. (In 1854 the Merchant Shipping Act required that all British sailors on pri-vate ships be provided with antiscorbutics, which usually meant lime juice.) Later, the nickname Limeys came to apply to all the English. The West Indian sour lime, however, is a source of ascor-bic acid far inferior to the Mediterranean lemon, although this was not known until the twentieth century. Sour limes contain only about a third of the ascorbic acid of oranges and lemons.

By the mid-nineteenth century, lime juice was being mass-produced in large quantities, not just for the Royal Navy but for the merchant marine and for shipping to America and Europe. Produc-tion was not tightly controlled, however, and inferior batches that were allowed to settle too long in holding tanks, were exposed to prolonged heat, or were run through copper pipes in the bottling process frequently found their way to market. Lime and lemon were then being used interchangeably, and it is impossible to know whether a supply was of lemon juice or the inferior lime. The daily ration of three-quarters of an ounce of lemon juice was itself barely adequate to ward off scurvy in the absence of fresh foods, and when that ration was replaced by lime juice with one-third the potency or less (depending on the manufacturing process) scurvy was bound to reappear on lengthy voyages or expeditions.

French troops suffered horribly from scurvy during their military campaign with Britain and Turkey against Russia in the Crimean War in the mid-1850s. Scurvy also appeared on several polar and Antarctic expeditions, and it undoubtedly killed many slaves on transport ships from Africa to the Americas. It was certainly common on the ships that transported thousands of British convicts to Australia, although in the absence of accurate medical reports, it would be impossible to disentangle the impact of scurvy from that of other diseases, such as tuberculosis, yellow fever, infections, or even malaria. Scurvy regularly appeared in prisons and in prisoner-of-war camps into the twentieth century when there were insufficient food supplies, and it was a frequent ailment of troops in the American Civil War, between 1861 and 1865. It ran rampant during the California Gold Rush, between 1848 and 1850, and made an appearance in the late nineteenth century in infants of wealthy families in Europe and America, when women switched from breast-feeding to the newly fashionable bottles of condensed milk, or when babies were weaned and then fed on a diet of oatmeal or other mashed grains. The condensed milk contained no vitamin C, and the symptoms were frequently misdiagnosed as rickets.

The key difference between the nineteenth-century occurrences of land scurvy and scurvy during the Age of Sail was that none of these later incidences had any significant impact on global events. As well, the cure was generally known, even though it might have been temporarily unavailable. Nevertheless, when the disease reappeared, it gave rise to some interesting debate and questions as theorists, researchers, and physicians sought again to more clearly define it. Each outbreak of scurvy sparked new theories that looked for the causative agent behind it: a lack of protein, a lack of potassium, bacterial infection, excessive acidity in the blood, ptomaine poisoning from tinned meat, excessive heat in the sterilization of milk, self-poisoning from blocked bowels, etc. Even though scurvy was no longer a complete mystery, it was still not understood—indeed it was not possible to truly understand the nature of the disease with nineteenth-century technology. The endless debate was not resolved until the early twentieth century, when new discoveries in nutrition began to raise the possibility of a negative factor for scurvy—that is, that it was caused by a lack of something.

With advancements in chemistry and more rigorous scientific method, theories could more easily be proved or disproved. Between 1907 and 1912, two Norwegian researchers, Axel Holst and Theodor Frolich, discovered that guinea pigs fed a diet of grain developed symptoms similar to scurvy and then died. They showed that when they added fresh vegetables and fruit—the same substances considered antiscorbutic in humans—the scurvy symptoms disappeared. It was a remarkable achievement: they had shown that scurvy could be induced by diet and eliminated by diet. Since almost all animals produce their own ascorbic acid internally and are immune to scurvy, Holst and Frolich's use of guinea pigs was particularly fortunate, and the discovery of a suitable test animal greatly sped up the process of isolating the active antiscorbutic agent in fresh foods and citrus juice.

There were a great number of studies looking into scurvy and its complex chemistry after the First World War. Yet it was not until 1932 that the active antiscorbutic compound was isolated by a Hungarian scientist, Albert Szent-Gyorgyi, while he was working at the University of Cambridge. He called it hexuronic acid, and it was later renamed ascorbic acid, after "antiscorbutic." In 1933, a Swiss team headed by Tadeus Reichstein and an English team headed by Sir Norman Haworth rushed to understand and decipher the molecular structure of the acid. They were both successful. In 1937, Szent-Gyorgyi was awarded a Nobel Prize in physiology and medicine and Sir Norman Haworth was awarded a Nobel Prize in Chemistry, partly for their work on vitamin C. Reichstein devised a method for synthesizing the acid commercially, and vitamin C is now a common food additive, easily and cheaply available.

Knowledge and technology have converged to eliminate scurvy from the daily lives of much of the world. Not only is synthetic ascorbic acid common, but refrigeration and canning can preserve foods for months or even years. In spite of the availability of synthetic ascorbic acid and vitamin C–fortified foods, however, scurvy will always be with us. It is not a disease that can be vaccinated against. It will arise anywhere and anytime diet is insufficient in ascorbic acid. Hundreds of thousands of people worldwide routinely suffer from scurvy—during droughts, the wet season, the dry season, when food distribution networks are disrupted by wars or natural disasters, and in refugee camps. Wherever there is famine, scurvy will be one of the handful of deficiency diseases that run rampant. Even in the wealthy democracies of the Western world, scurvy occasionally crops up in people who eat extremely poorly balanced diets or those who eat only junk food.

But after the defeat of Napoleon in 1815, scurvy was never again a determiner of global history. The clash between France and England during the Napoleonic Wars was the climax of scurvy's influence on world affairs, when it could cripple entire navies and hold the survival of nations in the balance. With the development of steam power in the mid-nineteenth century, which liberated mariners from the whim of the wind and the need for long detours chasing favourable currents, ships spent far less time at sea between ports and the illness faded for good, as an occupational disease for sailors, into the pages of history.

Many historians have commented on the strange and peculiar story of the quest for scurvy's cure, and on the improbability of such a seemingly simple solution requiring such a long time to discover. "Perhaps one of the most bewildering aspects of the history of scurvy," wrote J. J. Keevil in 1957, "is the manner in which a cure was repeatedly found, only to be lost again because of a wrong theory of its manner of operation, or because some uncontrollable factor offered a preferable explanation when it came to accounting for deaths." K. J. Carpenter commented in 1985 on how medical theorists and academics got in the way of a practical cure that was at one time common and accepted. "It is a humbling moral to the story," he wrote, "that, after all the attempts to apply new scientific concepts and hypothesis, the final solution came from rejection of theory and a return to the practical experience of previous centuries." In 1936, F. M. R. Walshe wrote that "the Lords of the Admiralty, concerned at the existence of an agency more effective than the enemies' guns and with a deference for hygiene characteristic of all military bodies, adopted Lind's recommendations for the Navy after an interval of only forty years." After only forty years! Tens of thousands of men died in that interval, and Lind's method for creating the rob was flawed anyway. It seems that Walshe must have had a keen sense of irony, in light of the Admiralty's stubborn ignorance of hygienic matters for most of the eighteenth century and the almost painfully convoluted and roundabout path that finally led to scurvy's being vanquished. But perhaps he was indeed being earnest. After all, the French and Spanish navies didn't solve the problem despite the comparative ease with which they might have obtained lemons and the equally compelling motivation of national defence and military conquest.

But it was Gilbert Blane, writing a decade before his death, long after scurvy had ceased to be a major problem for the Royal Navy, whose commentary expressed a timeless wisdom that transcends the theatre of warfare and nationalism within which he wrote it.

Indeed, it is an observation that applies to a good many aspects of human endeavour and to society in general. "There is not probably to be found in the whole range of human affairs," he wrote, referring to the eradication of scurvy following the introduction of the daily ration of lemon juice in 1795, "a finer illustration of the practical benefits of progressive knowledge in promoting the great interests of mankind: so that science, while it lends an aid, also sheds a grace and dignity over the useful arts: nor can there be a more striking proof of the maxim, that humanity, like every other mortal virtue, is the best policy."

Appendix

Vitamin C Contained in Common Foods
of the Age of Sail

———————————————

Substance	Mg per 100 g
Fruits	
Lemon juice	50–80
Lemon rob (fresh)	240
Lemon rob after a month's storage	60
Orange juice	50–80
Medium oranges	50
Lime juice	20–30
Grapefruits	37–50
Papayas	30–120
Peaches	less than 10
Mangoes	10–50
Plums	less than 10
Pineapples	20–60
Strawberries	40–90
Apples	10 or less
Apple cider	trace
Blackberries	15
Grapes	less than 10

Bananas	less than 10
Gooseberries	50–65

Vegetables

Onions (raw)	5–32
Onions (cooked)	2–3
Sauerkraut (after one month)	10
Parsley	140
Scurvy grass (spoonwort)	50–200
Dried peas	trace
Conifer needles	30–270
Conifer needles (fresh infusion)	14–100
Conifer needles (fermented, aged)	less than 0.5
Spinach	50–90
Potatoes (raw)	10–30
Potatoes (cooked)	5–15
Lettuce	6–18
Cauliflower	70–80
Broccoli	90–150
Carrots	10 or less
Tomatoes	10–40
Rice	0
Fresh bread	0
Grains	0

Meats

Fresh meat	trace
Cooked meat	0
Liver	10–40
Kidney	10–40

Other

Sugar	o
Vinegar	o
Coffee	o
Alcohol	o
Molasses	o
Milk	o
Malt (wort of malt)	o–trace

(Based on Hughes, 1951; Lloyd and Coulter, 1961; Carpenter, 1986; Cuppage, 1994)

Timeline

1492: Christopher Columbus first crosses the Atlantic from Spain to the Caribbean, beginning the great era of European exploration and the Age of Sail.

1497–98: First outbreak of scurvy on a naval voyage is recorded by the Portuguese captain Vasco da Gama while sailing around the Cape of Good Hope.

1519–22: Ferdinand Magellan's expedition suffers horribly from scurvy during the first circumnavigation of the world.

1534–35: The French explorer Jacques Cartier and some of his crew survive scurvy with the help of the Iroquois while wintering along the St. Lawrence.

1577: Francis Drake records one of several incidents of scurvy during his life at sea.

1586: Thomas Cavendish claims that scurvy is caused by "an infection of the blood and liver."

1588: Scurvy strikes the Spanish Armada during the failed invasion of England.

1591: John Davis leads a voyage to the South Seas and suffers from scurvy in the Straits of Magellan.

1593: First recorded use of lemons to "cure" scurvy by Sir Richard Hawkins.

1601: James Lancaster defeats scurvy on board the *Red Dragon* on the first East India Company voyage.

1601–30s: "Lemon water" juice is a common scurvy preventative on East India Company voyages. Mariners of the Dutch East India Company use rations of citrus juice and grow gardens on their ships.

1605: The French naval surgeon Lescarbot blames scurvy on poor food.

1630s: The East India Company begins issuing tamarinds and oil of vitriol for scurvy instead of citrus juice. Mariners die horribly as the cure is lost.

1668–1738: The famous Dutch physician Hermann Boerhaave theorizes that scurvy is the result of an imbalance in the bodily humours.

1701–13: The War of the Spanish Succession rages between England and Spain.

1716: James Lind is born.

1730s: Johan Friedrich Bachstrom claims that scurvy is a deficiency disease cured by fresh vegetables and fruits. He is ignored because his claim runs counter to prevailing theory.

1735: Lind is appointed head of Haslar hospital. Carolus Linnaeus publishes his *Systema Naturae*.

1736: The English naval surgeon William Cockburn claims that scurvy is caused by idleness hindering digestion.

1739–41: The War of Jenkins's Ear erupts between England and Spain. Lind enters the Royal Navy.

1740–44: Commodore George Anson circumnavigates the globe and captures the Spanish treasure galleon off the Philippines. Only two hundred or so of his original two thousand men survive, with over 90 percent dying of scurvy. The terrible loss heralds a golden age of scurvy research in England.

1740–48: The War of the Austrian Succession erupts between European allies, with France and England on opposing sides.

1747: Aboard the *Salisbury* in the English Channel, Lind conducts the first controlled trial in medical history and determines that citrus juice is "a virtual specific" for scurvy.

1749: Gilbert Blane is born.

1751: Sir George Anson is appointed First Lord of the Admiralty.

1753: Lind's *Treatise on the Scurvy*, dedicated to Lord Anson, is published and ignored. The Royal Navy orders all ships to be supplied with Ward's Drop and Pill, a violent purgative, as an antiscorbutic. Anthony Addington publishes *An Essay on the Sea Scurvy*, in which he advocates using sea water and bloodletting as scurvy cures.

1755: The beginning of the Seven Years' War, with England and France on opposing sides. Samuel Johnson's dictionary is published. Charles Bisset releases *A Treatise on the Scurvy*, in which he recommends alcohol, sugar, and rice as antiscorbutics.

1757: Lind publishes his *Essay on the Most Effecual Means of Preserving the Health of Seamen in the Royal Navy*, the second edition of the *Treatise on the Scurvy*.

1762: Sir George Anson dies, bringing to an end Lind's support within the Admiralty.

1763: The end of the Seven Years' War.

1764: David MacBride publishes the first edition of his *Experimental Essays*, in which he advocates wort of malt as an antiscorbutic.

1766: Samuel Wallis's Pacific expedition suffers from scurvy at Tahiti and fails to conduct valid antiscorbutic trials.

1766–69: Louis Antoine de Bougainville voyages to Tahiti and suffers scurvy in the Pacific.

1768: Lind publishes his *Essay on Diseases Incidental to Europeans in Hot Climates*.

1768–71: Lieutenant James Cook leads his first voyage of discovery and defeats scurvy, but he is unsure of the most effective cure.

1772: Sir John Pringle, president of the Royal Society, favours wort of malt over citrus juice as an antiscorbutic. The third edition of Lind's treatise is published.

1772–75: Cook makes his second voyage and appears to endorse wort of malt as the most effective antiscorbutic.

1775–83: The War of American Independence is fought.

1776–81: Cook's third voyage takes place.

1778: France joins the rebelling American colonies against England. Scurvy becomes a terrible problem in the Royal Navy. Joseph Banks becomes president of the Royal Society, replacing Sir John Pringle.

1779: Cook is killed in Hawaii. A combined French and Spanish fleet fails to invade England because of scurvy.

1780: Gilbert Blane publishes *A Short Account of the Most Effectual Means of Preserving the Health of Seamen* and becomes physician to the West Indies fleet under Admiral Sir George Rodney.

1781: General Cornwallis surrenders to George Washington at the Battle of Yorktown after the French fleet keeps the British fleet engaged and unable to aid him.

1782: The Royal Navy enjoys a staggering victory against a larger French fleet at the Battle of the Saints; in the months before the battle, Blane virtually eliminates scurvy in the British fleet. James Watt invents the double-acting rotary steam engine. The Montgolfier brothers design the first hot-air balloon.

1783: Lind resigns as the head of Haslar hospital and retires at the age of sixty-seven. William Wilberforce and Thomas Clarkson argue for the abolition of the slave trade.

1794: The aging English mariner William Hutchinson claims that salty food is the cause of scurvy and a daily cup of tea is the cure. James Lind dies.

1793–1815: The Royal Navy maintains a naval blockade of French ports for nearly the entire French Revolution and Napoleonic Wars, preventing French troops from invading England.

1795: Sir Gilbert Blane persuades the British Admiralty to issue a daily ration of lemon juice to all sailors, virtually eliminating scurvy aboard navy ships.

1797: Napoleon begins constructing barges in northern France for the invasion of England.

1799: Napoleon becomes the master of France and dominates Europe.

1804: Napoleon crowns himself emperor.

1805: The Battle of Trafalgar establishes the effectiveness of the Royal Navy blockade in preventing Napoleon's navy from controlling the English Channel and allowing the invasion of England.

1808: The American navy begins issuing lemon juice on long voyages.

1834: Sir Gilbert Blane dies. The Spanish Inquisition is finally suppressed.

1840s: Scurvy breaks out during the Crimean War, particularly amongst the French troops.

1847: Scurvy develops during the Irish potato famine.

1849: Scurvy develops during the California Gold Rush.

1867: The Scottish merchant Lauchlan Rose begins marketing sweetened lime juice to the public as Rose's Lime Juice Cordial, the world's first soft drink. Lime juice becomes a legal requirement for ships of the merchant marine in Britain.

1883: Infantile scurvy is first described by Thomas Barlow.

1907–12: Scurvy is produced in guinea pigs by Axel Holst and Theodor Frolich.

1912: Casimir Funk, at the Lister Institute in London, coins the term "vitamin" to describe vital nutritional components of food.

1932: Albert Szent-Gyorgyi first isolates ascorbic acid.

1933: Swiss and British teams independently decipher the molecular structure of ascorbic acid for synthetic reproduction.

A Note on Sources
and Further Reading

Because this is intended as a popular rather than scholarly book, I have elected not to include footnotes in the text. Following is a chapter-by-chapter discussion of my main sources for each section, with emphasis on those that would be useful for anyone wishing to learn more on a given topic. A complete bibliography of key specific and general sources follows. Important contributors are referenced in the bibliography.

Chapter One—The Eighteenth-Century Seafaring World: The Age of Scurvy

Books of interest on the life of sailors include *Men-of-War: Life in Nelson's Navy* by Patrick O'Brian and Gilbert Blane's *Essay on the Most Effectual Means of Preserving the Health of Seamen in the Royal Navy*, in *The Health of Seamen: Selections from the Works of Dr. James Lind, Sir Gilbert Blane and Dr. Thomas Trotter*, edited by Christopher Lloyd. One of the most interesting books to discuss food on ships during the Age of Sail is *Pickled, Potted and Canned: The Story of Food Preserving* by Sue Shephard. Also see *The Wooden World: An Anatomy of the*

Georgian Navy by N. A. M. Rodger. There are many other books that detail life in the navy during the Age of Sail, and a search of a good library should reveal several.

Chapter Two—Scurvy: The Plague of the Sea

An excellent referenced summary of early incidents of scurvy on voyages dating back to the sixteenth century can be found in the second volume of J. J. Keevil's monumental *Medicine and the Navy*. Richard Hakluyt's *Principal Navigations Voyages Traffiques and Discoveries of the English Nation* contains numerous first-hand accounts of the early English maritime expeditions. The varied publications of the Hakluyt Society provide reprinted and edited (and translated) accounts of most noteworthy early voyages of exploration or trade, from Francis Drake to François Pyrard to Jacques Cartier. Lind's treatise also lists all voyages where he found scurvy to be present, along with quotes from historical journals.

K. J. Carpenter's *History of Scurvy and Vitamin C* was particularly useful for understanding the chemical properties of vitamin C and the body's increased consumption rates under the stressful conditions inherent in a life at sea.

Chapter Three—Disaster and Victory in the South Seas: Lord Anson's Terrible Voyage

Anson's voyage is well documented. The best recent account is Glyn Williams's *Prize of All the Oceans: Commodore Anson's Daring Voyage and the Triumphant Capture of the Spanish Treasure Galleon*. Anson's own account of the voyage, *A Voyage Round the World in the Years 1740, 41, 42, 43, 44*, and the journals of Lieutenant Philip Saumarez (edited by Leo Heaps) are also vital and interesting.

A Note on Sources and Further Reading

Chapter Four—Found and Lost: The Search for a Cure Begins

Information on the early voyages of merchants of the East India Company include Richard Hawkins's *Voyage into the South Sea, in the Year 1593* and James Lancaster's *Voyage of James Lancaster to Brazil and the East Indies*, edited by W. Foster, both reprinted by the Hakluyt Society. One of many good introductions to the discovery and loss of a scurvy cure by the East India Company in the seventeenth century can be found in Karl Vogel's essay "Scurvy: The Plague of the Sea and the Spoyle of Mariners" in the *Bulletin of the New York Academy of Medicine*.

A summary of the many early theories on scurvy, including Bachstrom's and Boerhaave's, is found in Lind's treatise, while a basic book on the history of medicine, such as Erwin Heinz Ackerknecht's *Short History of Medicine*, will explain the somewhat convoluted logic of the theory of the four bodily humours. Volume 3 of Christopher Lloyd and Jack Coulter's *Medicine and the Navy* highlights some of the peculiar recommendations from the medical establishment to the Royal Navy in the eighteenth century. See also Carpenter's *History of Scurvy and Vitamin C*, an excellent general source, and Francisco Guerra's article "Hispanic-American Contribution to the History of Scurvy" in *Centaurus*.

Chapter Five—An Ounce of Prevention: James Lind and the *Salisbury* Experiment

Although somewhat out of date, Louis H. Roddis's 1950 biography, *James Lind: Founder of Nautical Medicine*, is still the best detailed summary of Lind's life and career. And once again Lind's treatise is a fount of information relating to his pioneering experiment, eighteenth-century medical thinking in general, and his own philosophizing and speculations. "The Curious Obscurity of Dr. James Lind" by A. P. Meiklejohn in the *Journal of the History of Medicine and Allied Sciences* explores the animosity between Lind and two influential colleagues, Anthony Addington and Charles Bisset.

Chapter Six—Unwinding the Knot:
Rob and Wort and the Trials at Sea

The 1953 reprint of Lind's treatise contains informative biographical and technical information in supplementary essays by the editors and other Lind scholars. It also contains a letter that Lind wrote resigning his position as treasurer of the Royal College of Physicians of Edinburgh, which is the source for much of the information about the workings of Haslar hospital. An exploration of the effectiveness of some of Lind's recommended cures for scurvy, including his citrus rob, are to be found in R. E. Hughes's article "James Lind and the Cure for Scurvy: An Experimental Approach" in the journal *Medical History*. The theories of Pringle and MacBride are discussed in Lloyd and Coulter's *Medicine and the Navy*, vol. 3; in Sir James Watt's "Medical Aspects and Consequences of Cook's Voyages" (in *Captain James Cook and His Times*, edited by Robin Fisher and Hugh Johnson); in the article "Sir John Pringle and His Circle," by Dorothea Waley Singer, in the journal *Annals of Science*; as well as in several other general sources.

Chapter Seven—Master Mariner:
James Cook's Great Voyages in the Pacific

Cook's decade-long odyssey of discovery is one of the greatest tales in the annals of the history of exploration. Presented here is merely the briefest outline of the adventures, as they relate to scurvy. There are numerous excellent biographies of James Cook; however, John Cawte Beaglehole's annotated journals and biography should be the foundation for any serious further reading. A collection of essays by leading scholars, *Captain*

James Cook and His Times, edited by Robin Fisher and Hugh Johnson, is an excellent and varied selection of Cook-related information. The recently published *Blue Latitudes: Boldly Going Where Captain Cook Has Gone Before* by T. Horwitz is an intriguing modern travel account tracing Cook's voyages and providing insights into his personality and character.

Chapter Eight—Man of Influence: Gilbert Blane and the West Indies Fleet

Although there is no biography of Sir Gilbert Blane, there are numerous articles that at least give a basic outline of his life and career. Two good places to begin are A. W. Beasely's article in the *Annals of the Royal College of Surgeons of England* and J. S. Taylor's "Founders of Naval Hygiene: Lind, Trotter, and Blane" in the *United States Naval Medicine Bulletin*.

Blane's own writings (*A Short Account of the Most Effectual Means of Preserving the Health of Seamen* and *Observations on the Diseases Incident to Seamen*, contained in Lloyd's *Health of Seamen: Selections from the Works of Dr. James Lind, Sir Gilbert Blane and Dr. Thomas Trotter*) are also particularly revealing, and give detailed arguments and statistics on the state of scurvy and other diseases in the West Indies fleet. See Lloyd and Coulter's *Medicine and the Navy*, vol. 3, for details of the horrendous state of the Channel fleet during the American War of Independence. See Sir James Watt's "Medical Aspects and Consequences of Cook's Voyages" and Beaglehole's annotated edition of Cook's and Banks's journals for primary information on the debate over wort of malt and citrus rob. Books on naval strategy during the late eighteenth century and during the War of American Independence are numerous; one good source is Paul Kennedy's *Rise and Fall of British Naval Mastery*. Another is Richard Harding's *Seapower and Naval Warfare, 1650–1830*.

Chapter Nine—Blockade: The Defeat of Scurvy and Napoleon

Harding's *Seapower and Naval Warfare* is one of a number of good
general sources for information on the naval blockade during
the Napoleonic era. See Christopher Lloyd's *Nelson and Sea
Power* for a good, brief outline of Nelson's life and accomplishments (there are dozens of biographies of Nelson). Numerous
general books detail the particulars of Nelson-era sea battles
and naval strategy, and these can include a bewildering array
of battle and tactical particulars beyond the scope of this book
(such as the influence of winds and currents, a comparison
of different gun types and firing techniques, and an analysis of
sailing styles and differences in the overall national naval strategy). Warfare during the height of the Age of Sail was extremely
complex and, in many cases, difficult to comprehend, focused
as it was on such things as gaining the "weather gauge" or antic-
ipating an opponent's response to wind and tide. Presented
here are only the known particulars of a battle's outcome, not
any explanation of how that outcome was affected by the
actions of commanders or weather. Even analyzing the specific
effect of diseases like scurvy on fighting and sailing ability
is difficult because usually no accurate records exist. A good
place to start, however, is with H. P. Willmott's *Sea Warfare:
Weapons, Tactics and Strategy* or Brian Tunstall and Nicholas
Tracy's *Naval Warfare in the Age of Sail: The Evolution of Fighting Tactics, 1680–1815*.

Lloyd and Coulter, in *Medicine and the Navy*, vol. 3, detail
the quantity of lemon juice issued by the Royal Navy after
1795, while Blane, in *Observations on the Diseases Incident to
Seamen*, provides statistics on the occurrence of scurvy during
the French Revolution and the Napoleonic Wars, as well as
statistics and anecdotes detailing the remarkable disappearance
of scurvy after 1795. Paul Kennedy's *Rise and Fall of the Great
Powers* compares the Royal Navy with the French and Spanish

navies, and provides an overview of the economic and social conditions that contributed to the elevation of Britain to pre-eminent naval and world power during the nineteenth century. Much has been written on this subject, and a good library should contain several sources discussing the rise of the British Empire.

Epilogue: The Mystery Solved

The recurrence of scurvy after the Napoleonic Wars is covered in detail in Carpenter's *History of Scurvy and Vitamin C*, which places particular emphasis on the many varied theories that arose after specific outbreaks. It also details the somewhat convoluted story of the chemists of the early twentieth century. See also the scholarly essays in the 1953 edition of Lind's treatise (edited by C. P. Stewart and D. Guthrie) for a detailed history of the chemistry of ascorbic acid and a discussion of the occurrence of scurvy on Arctic and polar expeditions. Sue Shephard's *Pickled, Potted and Canned: The Story of Food Preserving* discusses the nineteenth-century revolution in canning and the problems with condensed milk.

Bibliography

Ackerknecht, Erwin Heinz. *A Short History of Medicine*. Baltimore: Johns Hopkins University Press, 1982.

Anson, George. *A Voyage Round the World in the Years 1740, 41, 42, 43, 44*. London: Ingram, Cooke and Co., 1853 reprint.

Beaglehole, John Cawte. *The Life of Captain James Cook*. Stanford: Stanford University Press, 1974.

Beaglehole, John Cawte. ed. *The* Endeavour *Journal of Joseph Banks, 1768–1771*. Sydney: Library of New South Wales, 1962.

———. *The Journals of Captain James Cook on His Voyages of Discovery*. Millwood, NY: Hakluyt Society, 1988.

Beasely, A. W. "Sir Gilbert Blane." *Annals of the Royal College of Surgeons of England* 67 (1985): 332–33.

Biggar, H. P. *The Voyages of Jacques Cartier*. Ottawa: Acland, 1924.

Carpenter, Kenneth J. *The History of Scurvy and Vitamin C*. Cambridge: Cambridge University Press, 1986.

Chamier, Frederick. *The Life of a Sailor*. London: R. Bentley, 1832.

Cuppage, Francis E. *James Cook and the Conquest of Scurvy*. Westport, CN: Greenwood Press, 1994.

Dickman, S. R. "The Search for the Specific Factor in Scurvy." *Perspectives in Biology and Medicine* 24 (1981): 382–95.

Fisher, Robin, and Hugh Johnson, eds. *Captain James Cook and His Times.* Seattle: University of Washington Press, 1979.

Foster, W., ed. *The Voyage of James Lancaster to Brazil and the East Indies (1591–1603).* London: Hakluyt Society, 1940.

Glass, J. "James Lind, M.D., Eighteenth-Century Naval Medical Hygienist: Part 1. Biographical Notes with an Appreciation of the Naval Background." *Journal of the Royal Navy Medical Service* 35 (1949): 1–20.

———. "James Lind, M.D., Eighteenth-Century Naval Medical Hygienist: Part 2. Biographical Notes with an Appreciation of the Naval Background." *Journal of the Royal Navy Medical Service* 35 (1949): 68–86.

Gordon, E. C. "Scurvy and Anson's Voyage Round the World: 1740–1744. An Analysis of the Royal Navy's Worst Outbreak." *American Neptune* 44 (1984): 155–66.

Gray, Albert, ed. *The Voyage of François Pyrard.* London: Hakluyt Society, 1887.

Guerra, Francisco. "Hispanic-American Contribution to the History of Scurvy." *Centaurus* 1 (1950): 12–23.

Hakluyt, Richard. *The Principal Navigations Voyages Traffiques and Discoveries of the English Nation* (1589). Reprint. Cambridge: Hakluyt Society, 1965.

Harding, Richard. *Seapower and Naval Warfare, 1650–1830.* Maryland: Naval Institute Press, 1999.

Hattendorf, John B. *Mahan on Naval Strategy: Selections from the Writings of Rear Admiral Alfred Thayer Mahan.* Annapolis, MD: Naval Institute Press, 1991.

Hawkins, Richard. *Voyage into the South Sea, in the Year 1593* (1622). Reprint. London: Hakluyt Society, 1847.

Heaps, Leo, ed. *Log of the* Centurion: *Based on the Original Papers of Captain Philip Saumarez on Board* HMS Centurion, *Lord Anson's Flagship during his Circumnavigation, 1740–1744.* London: Hart-Davis, MacGibbon, 1973.

Horwitz, T. *Blue Latitudes: Boldly Going Where Captain Cook Has Gone Before.* New York: Henry Holt and Company, 2001.

Hudson, E., and A. Herbert. "James Lind: His Contribution to Shipboard Sanitation." *Journal of the History of Medicine and Allied Sciences* (Jan. 1956): 1–12.

Hughes, R. E. "James Lind and the Cure for Scurvy: An Experimental Approach." *Medical History* 19 (1951): 342–51.

Hutchinson, William. *A Treatise on Naval Architecture.* Liverpool: T. Billinge, 1794.

Keevil, J. J. *Medicine and the Navy, 1200–1900,* 2 vols. Edinburgh: E. and S. Livingstone Ltd., 1958.

Kennedy, Paul. *The Rise and Fall of the Great Powers: Economic Change and Military Conflict from 1500 to 2000.* New York: Random House, 1987.

———. *The Rise and Fall of British Naval Mastery.* London: Allen Lane, 1976.

Kippis, A. *A Narrative of the Voyages Round the World Performed by Captain James Cook.* Philadelphia: Porter and Coates, 1925.

Lloyd, Christopher. "The Introduction of Lemon Juice as a Cure for Scurvy." *Bulletin of the History of Medicine* 35 (1961): 123–32.

———. *Nelson and Sea Power.* London: The English Universities Press, Ltd., 1973.

Lloyd, Christopher, ed. *The Health of Seamen: Selections from the Works of Dr. James Lind, Sir Gilbert Blane and Dr. Thomas Trotter.* London: Navy Records Society, 1965.

Lloyd, Christopher, and Jack L. S. Coulter. *Medicine and the Navy, 1200–1900,* vols. 3 and 4. Edinburgh: E. and S. Livingstone Ltd., 1961.

Meiklejohn, A. P. "The Curious Obscurity of Dr. James Lind." *Journal of the History of Medicine and Allied Sciences* 9 (1954): 304–10.

O'Brian, Patrick. *Men-of-War: Life in Nelson's Navy.* New York: W. W. Norton, 1995.

Purchas, Samuel. *Purchas His Pilgrimes.* Glasgow: Hakluyt Society, 1906.

Roddis, Louis H. "The Influence of Scurvy upon Maritime History." *Military Surgeon* 86 (1940): 444–52.

———. *James Lind: Founder of Nautical Medicine.* New York: Henry Schuman, Inc., 1950.

Rodger, N. A. M. *The Wooden World: An Anatomy of the Georgian Navy.* London: William Collins and Sons, 1986.

Rolleston, Humphrey Davy. "Sir Gilbert Blane, M.D., F.R.S.: An Administrator of Naval Medicine and Hygiene." *Journal of the Royal Naval Medical Service* 2 (1916): 72–81.

Scott, Sir Harold H. *A History of Tropical Medicine,* vol. 2. London: Edward Arnold and Co., 1939.

Shephard, Sue. *Pickled, Potted and Canned: The Story of Food Preserving.* London: Headline Book Publishing, 2000.

Singer, Dorothea Waley. "Sir John Pringle and His Circle." *Annals of Science* 6 (1949–50): 127–80, 229–61.

Stewart, C. P., and Douglas Guthrie, eds. *Lind's Treatise on Scurvy.* Edinburgh: Edinburgh University Press, 1953.

Stockman, Ralph. "James Lind and Scurvy." *Edinburgh Medical Journal* 33 (1926): 329–50.

Taylor, J. S. "The Founders of Naval Hygiene: Lind, Trotter, and Blane." *United States Naval Medicine Bulletin* 14 (1920): 563–628.

Trotter, Thomas. *Medica Nautica: An Essay on the Diseases of Seamen.* London: Longman, 1804.

Tunstall, Brian, and Nicholas Tracy, eds. *Naval Warfare in the Age of Sail: The Evolution of Fighting Tactics, 1680–1815.* London: Conway Maritime Press, 1990.

Vogel, Karl. "Scurvy: The Plague of the Sea and the Spoyle of Mariners." *Bulletin of the New York Academy of Medicine* 9 (1933): 459–83.

Walshe, F. M. R. "Vitamin C." *University College Hospital Magazine* (Mar./Apr. 1936): 11.

Watt, James. "Medical Aspects and Consequences of Cook's Voyages." In *Captain James Cook and His Times*, edited by Robin Fisher and Hugh Johnson. Seattle: University of Washington Press, 1979.

Watt, J., E. J. Freeman, and W. F. Bynum. *Starving Sailors: The Influence of Nutrition upon Naval and Maritime History*. London: National Maritime Museum, 1981.

Williams, Glyn. *The Expansion of Europe in the Eighteenth Century: Overseas Rivalry, Discovery, and Exploitation*. London: Blandford Press, 1966.

———. *The Prize of All the Oceans: Commodore Anson's Daring Voyage and the Triumphant Capture of the Spanish Treasure Galleon*. Harmondsworth, UK: Penguin Books, 1999.

Willmott, H. P. *Sea Warfare: Weapons, Tactics and Strategy*. Chichester, UK: Anthony Bird Publications Ltd., 1981.

Woodall, John. *The Surgeon's Mate*. London: Nicholas Bourne, 1639. Microfiche.

Acknowledgements

I would like to thank and acknowledge all the talented individuals who transformed this manuscript into a book: Patrick Crean, Gordon Robertson, Alastair Williams, Janice Weaver, Kathleen Richards, John Lightfoot, Gillian Watts, and Kelly Cattermole. Particular credit goes to my editors, Liz Kershaw at Summersdale Publishers, Pete Wolverton at St. Martin's Press, and especially Jim Gifford at Thomas Allen Publishers, for their insightful observations and suggestions, which tightened and strengthened the book immeasurably. I would also like to thank my agents, Frances and Bill Hanna, who did a remarkable job organizing and coordinating the project with publishers on both sides of the Atlantic.

Scurvy required a lot of reading and research. I appreciate the efforts of Helene Lafontaine at the Canmore Public Library for helping me to collect articles and books from around the country. Thanks also to the Canada Council for the Arts for giving me an artist's project grant.

This book could not have been completed without the patience and contributions of my wife, Nicky Brink. She encouraged me and lent her support from the moment I conceived of this project on a dreary November afternoon, when I was eating an orange and wondering how people acquired enough vitamin C before the advent of modern transportation and refrigeration, which brought fresh fruit to our doorsteps. Now that I know more about those distant times, I appreciate all the more my winter oranges.

Index

Index

Barton, William, 114
  battles, 93, 116. *See also specific battle*
    locations
battleships. *See* warships
beer, 18, 21, 40, 120
beriberi, 14, 125
Bering, Vitus, 32, 35
biscuit, 18, 19–20
Bisset, Charles, 107–9, 167
Blane, Gilbert, 6, 129, 170–76, 212
  on antiscorbutics, 174, 179–81, 200,
    201
  as fleet physician, 170–71, 175–77,
    197, 202
  later career of, 179–81
  on mariners, 23, 203, 205–6
  recognition of, 182–83
  social connections of, 171–72,
    175–76, 183–84
  in West Indies, 172–73
  writings of, 172–73, 179, 209, 216–17
bloodletting, 38, 107, 121
Boerhaave, Hermann, 80–81, 89
  influence of, 84–85, 104, 123–24
Bonaparte, Napoleon. *See* Napoleon
  Bonaparte
Bougainville, Louis Antoine de, 32,
  138–39
Bucentaure, 186–88
Byron, John, 122

Cabral, Pedro, 32, 74
Calder, Robert, 193
Camoens, Luis de, 35
Canada, 27–31, 134–36, 195
Cape Horn, 47–50, 59–61
Cape St. Vincent, Battle of, 186
Carpenter, K. J., 78–79, 216
carrot marmalade, 148, 155
Carteret, Philip, 125–26
Cartier, Jacques, 27–31, 39, 195

Cavendish, Thomas, 36, 52
cedar bark, 29–31
Celsus, 79
Centurion, 1–2, 48–50, 52, 61, 190. *See
  also* Anson, George
  scurvy on, 63–64, 65–68
Chalmers, George, 109
Chamier, Frederick, 15
Champlain, Samuel de, 32
cheese, 18, 21, 40
Chelsea pensioners, 53–54
China, 39, 66, 68
cider, 76, 96–97
citrus fruit. *See also specific fruits;* rob
  Blane on, 173, 179
  opinions about, 80, 105, 127, 456
  in scurvy experiments, 96–97
Clerke, James, 160
clinical trials, 103
  in eighteenth century, 124–25, 129,
    156
  by James Lind, 95–98, 103, 130
Clowes, William, 34, 37–38
Cockburn, William, 37
Columbus, Christopher, 31
Cook, James, 6, 129
  accomplishments of, 145, 151–52,
    160, 183
  death of, 158–60
  early career of, 134–36
  first voyage of, 132, 133–34, 137–45
  health of, 145, 157–58
  Pringle and, 166–69
  and Royal Navy, 132, 134
  and scurvy prevention, 32–33,
    136–37, 150, 153–56, 168
  second voyage of, 148–51
  third voyage of, 152, 156–60
copper, 21, 45–46, 141–42
Corbella, Antonio, 204
Cornwallis, Charles, 206–7

Index

ARCTIC CIRCLE

SIBERIA

N

ASIA

CHINA

JAPAN

MACAO

PHILIPPINES

NEW GUINEA

INDONESIA

New
Hebrides

Sam

Fiji Is.

New
Caledonia

AUSTRALIA
(NEW HOLLAND)

TASMANIA

NEW
ZEALAND

Indian

Ocean

Pacif